HEBREW-ENGLISH
ENGLISH-HEBREW
DICTIONARY AND PHRASEBOOK

HEBREW-ENGLISH
ENGLISH-HEBREW
DICTIONARY AND PHRASEBOOK

ISRAEL PALCHAN

HIPPOCRENE BOOKS, INC
New York

This book is dedicated to my wife Mila Palchan.

Third printing, 2006.

For information, address:
HIPPOCRENE BOOKS, INC.
171 Madison Ave.
New York, NY 10016
www.hippocrenebooks.com

ISBN 0-7818-0811-1

Printed in the United States of America.

CONTENTS

Preface 5
The Hebrew Alphabet 6
Pronunciation Rules 7
Abbreviations 7
A Very Basic Grammar 8
Hebrew–English Dictionary 17
English–Hebrew Dictionary 75
Hebrew Phrasebook 127
- Introductions 136
- Etiquette 137
- Exclamation Words 138
- Quick Reference 139
- Inquiries 142
- Language 146
- Family 147
- Religion 149
- Nationality 149
- Transportation 150
- Buying Tickets 150
- Air Travel 150
- Bus & Taxi 151
- The Car 154
- Accommodation 157
- Directions 160
- Food & Drink 164
- What's to See 169
- Communications 171
  - Telephone 171
  - Mail 172
- Bureaucracy 173
- Money & Finance 175
- Shopping 177
  - Clothes, Shoes & Accessories 179
- Tools 183

Contents

Health 185
Emergencies 187
Sports 190
Politics 191
Farms & Animals 193
  Farming 193
  Animals 194
The Weather 196
Numbers 198
  Cardinal numbers 198
  Ordinal numbers 200
  Fractions 200
Time & Date 202
Colors 207
Professions 208

PREFACE

Hebrew is one of the world's ancient languages. For the last 2,000 years Hebrew was not used as a spoken language, and only in the last 100 years has it become a living, spoken language in the State of Israel and for many Jews all over the world. **Hebrew is written from right to left**. The alphabet is comprised of 22 letters with no vowels.

This phrasebook has been designed for tourists and students learning Hebrew. The entries in this book are given in three forms: Hebrew, Hebrew transliteration and English, allowing everyone to express themselves in Hebrew without fully knowing the language.

The phrasebook includes topics especially useful for the tourist, including: accomodations, transportation, foreign exchange, shopping, law, health and more.

THE HEBREW ALPHABET

letter	name of letter	pronun-ciation	letter	name of letter	pronun-ciation
א	a'leph	–	ל	la'med	**l**
ב	beit	**b,v**	מ, ם*	mem	**m**
ג	gi'mel	**g**	נ, ן*	nun	**n**
ד	da'let	**d**	ס	sa'mekh	**s**
ה	hey	**h**	ע	a'yin	–
ו	vav	**v, u, o**	פ, ף*	pei	**p, f**
ז	za'in	**z**	צ, ץ*	tza'di	**ts**
ח	khet	**kh**	ק	kuf	**k**
ט	tet	**t**	ר	resh	**r**
י	yud	**y**	שׁ	shin	**sh**
כ, ך*	kaf	**k, kh**	שׂ	sin	**s**
			ת	tav	**t**

* way of writing the letter when it comes at the end of a word.

The letters בּ, כּ, פּ are always pronounced respectively: "**b**", "**k**", and "**p**" at the beginning of a word. At the end of a word they are always pronounced "**v**", "**kh**", and "**f**".

The vowel sounds "**a**", "**e**", "**i**", "**o**", and "**u**" are not represented in Hebrew by letters. Sometimes they are represented by diacritical marks written around the consonants they are to follow, but often no indication appears in the text at all. Here is a list of vowels in Hebrew (◻ represents a consonant):

	Name		Name	Sound
◻ָ	kamatz' gadol'	◻ַ	patakh'	**a**
◻ֵ	tzeire'	◻ֶ	segol'	**e**
◻ִי	khirik' gadol'	◻ִ	khirik'	**i**
◻וֹ	kholam'	◻ָ	kamatz' katan'	**o**
◻וּ ;◻ֹ	shuruk'	◻ֻ	kubutz'	**u**

"Kamatz katan" appears in a very limited number of words and the reader may pronounce the vowel as "**a**" except in the common word כָּל **(kol)** *adj.* **all.**

These two columns have no differences in their pronunciation in modern Hebrew. Different diacritical marks are used only for Hebrew grammatical purposes.

PRONUNCIATION RULES

Transliteration	Pronunciation	As in
a	a	t**a**r
ay	igh	h**igh**
ey	ey	th**ey**
e	e	p**e**t
i	ee	m**ee**t
o	oh	d**oo**r
u	u	b**oo**k
h	h	**h**elp
kh	kh	Ba**ch**
ts	ts	bi**ts**
"	signifies a slight pause after the letter as if two words are stuck together	mar"kiv' = mar + kiv' lif"ol' = lif + ol'
'	one apostrophe signifies placing the accent on the related syllable	

look (n.)	mabat'	מבט
summary	sikum'	סיכום

ABBREVIATIONS

(f.) – feminine
(m.) – masculine
(s.) – singular
(pl.) – plural
(adj.) – adjective
(adv.) – adverb
(n.) – noun
(pron.) – pronoun
(v.) – verb
(conj.) – conjunction

A VERY BASIC GRAMMAR

Words in Hebrew (nouns, verbs, adjectives, adverbs, pronouns) appear in two genders only: masculine & feminine.

• MASCULINE & FEMININE

Verbs, nouns and adjectives take different suffixes to indicate the masculine and feminine. (In the tables below the big letters represent prefixes or suffixes added to the root.)

Suffixes common to feminine singular: "ת" - "et", "ה" - "a".

Singular	Masculine		Feminine		English
Verb in present tense	kotev'	כותב	kote'vet	כותבת	write
Noun	katav'	כתב	kate'vet	כתבת	correspondent
Adjective	katuv'	כתוב	ktuva'	כתובה	written
Verb in past tense	katav'	כתב	katva'	כתבה	wrote

• PLURAL

To the masculine plural the suffix "ים" – "im" is added.

To the feminine plural the suffix "ות" – "ot" is added.

Words which describe both genders together appear in the masculine form.

boys and girls marry בנים ובנות מתחתנים

banim' uvanot' mitkhatnim'

For example:

Plural	Masculine		Feminine		English
Verb	kotvim'	כותבים	kotvot'	כותבות	are writing
Noun	katavim'	כתבים	katavot'	כתבות	correspondents
Adjective	ktuvim'	כתובים	ktuvot'	כתובות	written

- WORD ORDER

In Hebrew it is customary to place the adjective after the noun it describes. (In English the adjective is placed before the noun.)

big city	ir gdola'	עיר גדולה
first meeting	pgisha' rishona'	פגישה ראשונה
hot water	ma'im khamim'	מים חמים
harsh rain	geshem khazak'	גשם חזק
eastern wind	ru'akh mizrakhit'	רוח מזרחית
good meal	arukha' tova'	ארוחה טובה

- VERBS

There are seven verb structures, or groups, called "binyanim" – בנינים, which literally means "buildings". Each group represents a different addition to the verb root, and follows its own conjugation. Most of the verbs are based on 3 root letters, some contain 4 letters for the root.

The following table shows the name of each binyan, or verb group, and how it is formed from the root. For example, the first structure, *Paal'* – פעל, does not change from the root.

(□□□ indicates the verb root letters)

Paal' פעל □□□	*Piel'* פיעל □י□□	*Hif"il'* היפעל ה□□י□
Nif"al' ניפעל נ□□□	*Pual'* פועל □ו□□	*Huf"al'* הופעל הו□□□
	Hitpael' התפעל הת□□□	

In the present tense, verb forms change according to gender (masculine and feminine) and number (singular and plural). The following table shows typical examples of masculine, feminine, singular and plural present tense forms for 3 of the verb groups.

to dance – *lirkod'* – לרקוד (*Paal* – פעל) root – רקד

		masculine		feminine	
(s.)	dance(s), am/is dancing	*roked'*	רוקד	*roke'det*	רוקדת
(pl.)	dance, are dancing	*rokdim'*	רוקדים	*rokdot'*	רוקדות

to speak – *ledaber'* – לדבר (*Piel* – פיעל) root – דבר

		masculine		feminine	
(s.)	speak(s), am/is speaking	*medaber'*	מדבר	*medabe'ret*	מדברת
(pl.)	speak, are speaking	*medabrim'*	מדברים	*medabrot'*	מדברות

to put oneself at risk – *lehistaken'* – להסתכן
(*Hitpael* – התפעל) root – סכנ

		masculine		feminine	
(s.)	put(s), am/is putting...	*mistaken'*	מסתכן	*mistake'net*	מסתכנת
(pl.)	put, are putting...	*mistaknim'*	מסתכנים	*mistaknot'*	מסתכנות

For example, the verb 'to write' – *likhtov'* – לכתוב is conjugated in the present tense as follows:

I (m.) write	**kotev'**	כותב
I (f.) write	**kote'vet**	כותבת
you (m.) write	**kotev'**	כותב
you (f.) write	**kote'vet**	כותבת
he writes	**kotev'**	כותב
she writes	**kote'vet**	כותבת
we (m.) write	**kotvim'**	כותבים
we (f.) write	**kotvot'**	כותבות
you (pl.)(m.) write	**kotvim'**	כותבים
you (pl.)(f.) write	**kotvot'**	כותבות
they (m.) write	**kotvim'**	כותבים
they (f.) write	**kotvot'**	כותבות

For the past and future tenses, verb conjugation is formed by adding prefixes to the right side of the verb root and suffixes to the left side, according to the pronouns.

The table below shows the verb forms for the past and future tenses. Suffixes and prefixes are the same for all "binyanim".

		past tense		future tense	
I	*ani'*	□***ti'***	□תי	***e/a***□	א□
you (m.)	*ata'*	□***ta'***	□ת	***t***□*	ת□
you (f.)	*at*	□***t***	□ת	***t***□***i***	ת□י
he	*hu*	□	□	***y***□	י□
she	*hi*	□***a'***	□ה	***t***□	ת□
we	*anakh'nu*	□***nu***	□נו	***n***□	נ□
you (pl.)(m.)	*atem'*	□***tem***	□תם	***t***□***u***	ת□ו
you (pl.)(f.)	*aten'*	□***ten***	□תן	***t***□***u***	ת□ו
they	*hem'*	□***u***	□ו	***y***□***u***	י□ו

• PREPOSITIONS

Prepositions in Hebrew consist of one letter, added to the following word.

In these examples the ellipses relate to the following word.

to	**le.../la...**	...ל
into	**letokh'**	לתוך
to the plane	**lamatos'**	למטוס
as	**ke.../ka.../ki...**	...כ
well, properly	**kerauy'**	כראוי
when, while, as	**kaasher'**	כאשר
from	**mi.../me.../meha...**	...מ
from me	**mimeni**	ממני
from above	**milma'ala**	מלמעלה
and	**ve...; u...**	...ו
and also	**vegam'**	וגם
and she	**vehi'**	והיא
and what	**uma'**	ומה

• ARTICLES IN HEBREW

The definite article "the" has its Hebrew equivalent in "ה" – *ha'*. It is written and spelled together with the word to which it refers.

For example: a) the man – *haish'* – האיש
the woman – *haisha'* – האישה
the airplane – *hamatos'* – המטוס

The indefinite article "a"/"an" has no special equivalent in Hebrew. The word is simply written without an article.

For example: b) a man – *ish'* – איש
a woman – *isha'* – אישה
an airplane – *matos'* – מטוס

• PRONOUNS

Pronouns are used in Hebrew in a similar way to English. The difference is that the Hebrew is written from right to left.

I want to see you.	**ani' rotse' lir"ot' otkha'.**	אני רוצה לראות אותך.
This is not right!	**ze lo nakhon'!**	זה לא נכון!
She promised to herself.	**hi hivti'kha leatsma'.**	היא הבטיחה לעצמה.

Possesive pronouns, like adjectives, are placed after the appropriate nouns. (In English they are placed before.)

Example:

Give me your ticket.	**ten li et hakartis' shelkha'.**	תן לי את הכרטיס שלך.

Personal pronouns

I	**ani'**	אני
you (m.)	**ata'**	אתה
you (f.)	**at**	את
he	**hu**	הוא
she	**hi**	היא
you (m.)(pl.)	**atem'**	אתם
you (f.)(pl.)	**aten'**	אתן
they (m.)	**hem**	הם
they (f.)	**hen**	הן
me	**oti'**	אותי
you (m.)	**otkha'**	אותך
you (f.)	**otakh'**	אותך
him	**oto'**	אותו
her	**ota'**	אותה
us	**ota'nu**	אותנו
you (m.)(pl.)	**etkhem'**	אתכם
you (f.)(pl.)	**etkhen'**	אתכן
them (m.)	**otam'**	אותם

them (f.)	**otan'**	אותן
to me	**li**	לי
to you (m.)	**lekha'**	לך
to you (f.)	**lakh**	לך
to him	**lo**	לו
to her	**la**	לה
to us	**la'nu**	לנו
to you (m.)(pl.)	**lakhem'**	לכם
to you (f.)(pl.)	**lakhen'**	לכן
to them (m.)	**lahem'**	להם
to them (f.)	**lahen'**	להן

Possessive pronouns

of (somebody's)	**shel...**	של...
my, mine	**sheli'**	שלי
your, yours (m.)	**shelkha'**	שלך
your, yours (f.)	**shelakh'**	שלך
his	**shelo'**	שלו
her, hers	**shela'**	שלה
our, ours	**shela'nu**	שלנו
your, yours (m.)(pl.)	**shelakhem'**	שלכם
your, yours (f.)(pl.)	**shelakhen'**	שלכן
their, theirs (m.)	**shelahem'**	שלהם
their, theirs (f.)	**shelahen'**	שלהן

Demonstrative pronouns

this (m.)	**ze**	זה
this (f.)	**zot, zo**	זאת, זו
these (m.)(f.)	**ey'le, ey'lu**	אילה, אילו

Reflexive pronouns

to myself	**leatsmi'**	לעצמי
to yourself (m.)	**leatsmekha'**	לעצמך
to yourself (f.)	**leatsmekh'**	לעצמך
to himself	**leatsmo'**	לעצמו

to herself	**leatsma'**	לעצמה
to ourselves	**leatsmey'nu**	לעצמינו
to yourselves (m.)	**leatsmekhem'**	לעצמכם
to yourselves (f.)	**leatsmekhen'**	לעצמכן
to themselves		
(m.)	**leatsmam'**	לעצמם
(f.)	**latsman'**	לעצמן

• HOW TO FORM A QUESTION

The interrogative is formed by adding a question mark to the end of a sentence when written and by adding an inflection to appropriate words, when speaking. The sentence structure does not change.

For example:

You (m.)(s.) are going to the store.	Ata' holech' lakhanut'.	אתה הולך לחנות.
Are you going **to the store**?	Ata' holech' **lakhanut'**?	אתה הולך לחנות?
Are you **going** to the store?	Ata' **holech'** lakhanut'?	אתה הולך לחנות?

• HOW TO FORM A NEGATIVE STATEMENT OR QUESTION

The negative particle **lo'** is placed before the verb in the sentence.

You are not going to the store.	Ata' **lo'** holech' lakhanut'.	אתה לא הולך לחנות.
You are not going to the store?	Ata' **lo'** holech' lakhanut'?	אתה לא הולך לחנות?

HEBREW–ENGLISH DICTIONARY

א

father	av	אב
aorta	av haorkim'	אב העורקים
my father	a'ba	אבא
I'll check it	evdok' zot	אבדוק זאת
lost	avud'	אבוד
avocado	avoka'do	אבוקדו
watermelon	avati 'yakh	אבטיח
but	aval'	אבל
dust (n.)	avak'	אבק
powder	avka'	אבקה
legend	agada'	אגדה
thumb	agudal'	אגודל
nuts	egozim'	אגוזים
lake	agam'	אגם
agnostic	agnos'ti	אגנוסטי
pear	agas'	אגס
red (m.)	adom'	אדום
red (f.)	aduma'	אדומה
master, sir	adon'	אדון
polite (m.)	adiv	אדיב
polite (f.)	adiva'	אדיבה
human	adam'	אדם
reddish	adamdam'	אדמדם
soil	adama'	אדמה
on the contrary	ad'raba	אדרבא
love (n.)	ahava'	אהבה
beloved	ahuv'	אהוב
hi!	ahlan'!	אהלן!
or	o	או
August	o'gust	אוגוסט
lipstick	o'dem	אודם
tent	o'hel	אוהל
ear	o'zen	אוזן
auto, car	o'to	אוטו
bus	o'tobus	אוטובוס
automatic	otoma'ti	אוטומטי
automation	otoma'tsiya	אוטומציה
Oh my God!	oy vaavoy' li!	אוי ואבוי לי!
don't you dare	oy' vaavoy' lekha'	אוי ואבוי לך
enemy	oyev'	אויב
air	avir'	אויר
food	o'khel	אוכל
kosher food	o'khel kasher'	אוכל כשר
population	okhlusiya'	אוכלוסיה

perhaps	ulay'	אולי
nut	um	אום
unfortunate (m.)	umlal'	אומלל
unfortunate (f.)	umlala'	אומללה
art	omanut'	אומנות
university	univer'sita	אוניברסיטה
bicycle	ofana'im	אופניים
treasure	otsar'	אוצר
October	okto'ber	אוקטובר
light	or	אור
parking lights	orot' khanaya'	אורות חניה
regular lights	orot' namukhim'	אורות נמוכים
rice	o'rez	אורז
length	o'rekh	אורך
sign, letter	ot	אות
her	ota'	אותה
him	oto'	אותו
same thing	oto' davar'	אותו דבר
me	oti'	אותי
us	ota'nu	אותנו
then	az	אז
so what?	az ma?	אז מה?
reference	izkur'	אזכור
civics	ezrakhut'	אזרחות
civil	ezrakhi'	אזרחי
brother	akh	אח
one (m.)	ekhad'	אחד
one by one	ekhad' ekhad'	אחד אחד
every single one	ekhad' ekhad'	אחד אחד
one of them	ekhad' mihem'	אחד מהם
eleven	akhad' asar'	אחד עשר
several	akhadim'	אחדים
backwards	akho'ra, leakhor'	אחורה, לאחור
nurse	akhot'	אחות
my sister	akhoti'	אחותי
my brother	akhi'	אחי
uniform	akhid'	אחיד
other	akher'	אחר
afterwards, later	akhar' kakh	אחר כך
last	akharon'	אחרון
behind	akharey'	אחרי
after all	akharey' hakol'	אחרי הכל
after this	akharey' ze	אחרי זה
after	akharey', leakhar'	אחרי, לאחר
responsibility	akhrayut'	אחריות
others	akherim'	אחרים
otherwise	akhe'ret	אחרת
one (f.)	akhat'	אחת
atom	atom'	אטום
sealed	atum'	אטום

atheist	ateist'	אטיאסט
atmosphere	atmosfe'ra	אטמוספירה
island	i	אי
forbidden! impossible!	i-efshar'!	אי אפשר!
you never know	i-efshar' lada'at	אי אפשר לדעת
you can't rely on it	i-efshar' lismokh'	אי אפשר לסמוך
therefore	i-lekhakh	אי לכך
trade union	igud' miktsoi'	איגוד מקצועי
workers' union	igud' ovdim'	איגוד עובדים
which? *(m.)*	ey'ze?	איזה?
some sort of (m.), some kind of (m.)	ey'ze shehu'	איזה שהוא
which? *(f.)*	ey'zo?	איזו?
some kind of (f.)	ey'zo shehi'	איזו שהיא
some sort of (f.)	ey'zo shehi'	איזו שהיא
zone, region	ezor'	איזור
unification	ikhud'	איחוד
slow	iti'	איטי
butcher	itliz'	איטליז
how?	eykh?	איך?
as you please	eykh sheata' rotse'	איך שאתה רוצה
quality	ikhut'	איכות
do you care?	ikhpat' lekha'?	איכפת לך?
farmer	ikar'	איכר
one way or another	eykh' shehu'	איכשהו
these *(m., f.)*	ey'le, ey'lu	אילה, אילו
which? *(pl.)*	ey'lu?	אילו?
Eilat	eylat'	אילת
there isn't, there is/are not	eyn	אין
there is no choice	eyn brera'	אין ברירה
no matter	eyn davar'	אין דבר
never mind	eyn davar'	אין דבר
it's senseless	eyn ta'am	אין טעם
no exit	eyn yetsiya'	אין יציאה
one hasn't the strength	eyn ko'akh	אין כח
no entry	eyn knisa'	אין כניסה
you have no right	eyn lekha' rshut'	אין לך רשות
nothing to do	eyn ma laasot'	אין מה לעשות
no luck	eyn mazal'	אין מזל
there is no need	eyn tso'rekh	אין צורך
there is no way	eyn shum efsharut'	אין שום אפשרות
no problem	eyn shum baaya'	אין שום בעיה
there is no reason	eyn shum siba'	אין שום סיבה
there is no doubt	eyn shum safek'	אין שום ספק
I don't remember.	eyne'ni zokher'.	אינני זוכר.
where?	ey'fo?	איפה?

somewhere	ey'fo shehu'	איפה שהוא
occasion	iru'a	אירוע
person, man	ish	איש
woman	isha'	אישה
authorization	ishur'	אישור
personal	ishi'	אישי
but	akh	אך
eating	akhila'	אכילה
indeed	akhen'	אכן
youth hostel	akhsaniyat' no'ar	אכסניית נוער
to	el	אל
to all this	el kol ze	אל כל זה
don't	al	אל
don't worry!	al tid"ag'	אל תדאג
don't be like that!	al tihye' kaze'	אל תהיה כזה
don't do that!	al taase' zot	אל תעשה זאת
don't be afraid	al tefakhed'	אל תפחד
don't take!	al tikakh'	אל תקח
don't forget	al tishkakh'	אל תשכח
algorithm	algoritm'	אלגוריתם
god	elokim'	אלוהים
aluminum	aluminium	אלומיניום
alternator	alterna'tor	אלטרנטור
violent	alim'	אלים
diagonal	alakhson'	אלכסון
coral	almog'	אלמוג
unless	ilmale'	אלמלא
thousand	e'lef	אלף
alphabet	a'lef bet	אלף־בית
two thousand	alpa'im	אלפיים
thousandth	alpit'	אלפית
electronics	elektro'nika	אלקטרוניקה
God	Elokim'	אלקים
alkaline	alka'li	אלקלי
allergy	aler'gia	אלרגיה
mother	em	אם
if	im	אם
if so	im kakh	אם כך
my (his, her,...) mother	i'ma	אמא
ambulance	a'mbulance	אמבולנס
bath	amba'tiya	אמבטיה
is supposed to be	amur' lihyot'	אמור להיות
is supposed to do	amur' laasot'	אמור לעשות
brave (m.)	amits'	אמיץ
brave (f.)	amitsa'	אמיצה
saying	amira'	אמירה
real	amiti'	אמיתי
yes, indeed	omnam' ken	אמנם כן
middle	em'tsa	אמצע
last night	e'mesh	אמש

truth	emet′	אמת
we	anakh′nu	אנחנו
antibiotic	antibio′tika	אנטיביאוטיקה
antenna	ante′na	אנטנה
I	ani′	אני
I ask for	ani′ mevakesh′	אני מבקש
I'm afraid	ani′ mefakhed′	אני מפחד
I need	ani′ tsarikh′	אני צריך
I want	ani′ rotse′	אני רוצה
I want to ask	ani rotse′ lish"ol′	אני חצה לשאול
I want to buy	ani′ rotse′ liknot′	אני רוצה לקנות
pineapple	ananas′	אננס
men, people	anashim′	אנשים
it is forbidden!	asur′!	אסור!
supply (n.)	aspaka′	אספקה
nose	af	אף
no one	af ekhad′	אף אחד
no one wants	af ekhad′ lo rotse′	אף אחד לא רוצה
despite	af al pi she...	אף על פי ש...
never	af paam′, af pa′am lo	אף פעם, אף פעם לא
gray (m.)	afor′	אפור
gray (f.)	afora′	אפורה
even	afi′lu	אפילו
zero	e′fes	אפס
April	April′	אפריל
peach	afarsek′	אפרסק
possible	efshar′	אפשר
possibility	efsharut′	אפשרות
at	e′tsel	אצל
gun	ekdakh′	אקדח
climate	aklim′	אקלים
four	arbaa′	ארבעה
four days	arbaa′ yamim′	ארבעה ימים
fourteen	arbaa′ asar′	ארבעה עשר
forty	arbaim′	ארבעים
meal	arukha′	ארוחה
breakfast	arukhat′ bo′ker	ארוחת בוקר
dinner	arukhat′ e′rev	ארוחת ערב
lunch	arukhat′ tsohora′im	ארוחת צהריים
long	arokh′	ארוך
closet	aron′	ארון
clothes closet	aron′ bgadim′	ארון בגדים
wall closet	aron′ kir	ארון קיר
lion	ariye′	אריה
country	e′rets	ארץ
fire	esh	אש
woman	isha′	אשה
grapefruit (grapefruits)	eshkolit′ (eshkoliyot′)	אשכולית (אשכוליות)

wizard	ashaf′	אשף
garbage	ashpa′	אשפה
that	asher′	אשר
you (m.)	at	אתה
you (f.)	ata′	את
you see!	ata′ roe′!	אתה רואה!
athletics	atle′tika kala′	אתלטיקה קלה
yesterday	etmol′	אתמול
site	atar′	אתר

ב

in, on	be...	ב...
on a bus	beo′tobus	באוטובוס
on the red light (traffic)	beor′ adom′	באור אדום
in the morning	babo′ker	בבוקר
in a hospital	beveyt′ kholim′	בבית חולים
nonsense, lies	bablat′	בבל"ט
please	bevakasha′	בבקשה
bathing suit	be′ged yam	בגד ים
clothes	bgadim′	בגדים
openly	begalu′y	בגלוי
because of	biglal′	בגלל
for, in order to	biglal′ she...	בגלל ש...
material	bad	בד
in parallel (*action*)	bad bevad′	בד בבד
crystal	bedolakh′	בדולח
exactly	bediyuk′	בדיוק
exactly on time	bediyuk′ bazman′	בדיוק בזמן
joke	bdikha′	בדיחה
tin	bdil	בדיל
looking back on it	bediavad′	בדיעבד
tensely	bedrikhut′	בדריכות
usually	bede′rekh klal	בדרך כלל
gradually	behadraga′	בהדרגה
definitely	bahekhlet′	בהחלט
certainly not	behekhlet′ lo	בהחלט לא
bright	bahir′	בהיר
in accordance with	behet"em′ le...	בהתאם ל...
in the beginning	behatkhala′	בהתחלה
come here	bo he′na	בוא הנה
come on already	bo kvar	בוא כבר
let′s do it	bo naase′	בוא נעשה
come to	bo′u el...	בואו אל...
builder	bone′	בונה
doll	buba′	בובה
morning	bo′ker	בוקר
good morning	bo′ker tov	בוקר טוב
boor	bur	בור
screw (n.)	bo′reg	בורג

perfume (n.)	bo'sem	בושם
waste of time	bizbuz' zman	בזבוז זמן
carefully	bizhirut'	בזהירות
on time	bazman'	בזמן
next month	bekho'desh haba'	בחודש הבא
on the shore	bakhof'	בחוף
outside	bakhuts'	בחוץ
fellow	bakhur'	בחור
girl	bakhura'	בחורה
sure! really!	bekhayay'!	בחיי!
come on, you are kidding!	bekhaye'kha!	בחייך!
sickness	bkhila'	בחילה
exam	bkhina'	בחינה
hastily	bekhipazon'	בחיפזון
selection	bkhira'	בחירה
secretly	bekhashay'	בחשאי
on suspicion of	bekha'shad shel	בחשד של
in the long run	betvakh' arokh'	בטווח ארוך
in the short run	betvakh' katsar'	בטווח קצר
safely, sure	batu'akh	בטוח
sure	be'takh	בטח
safety	betikhut'	בטיחות
abdomen, stomach	be'ten	בטן
insulation	bidud'	בידוד
sewage	biyuv'	ביוב
biology	biolo'giya	ביולוגיה
on (day), during the day	bayom'	ביום
expensive	beyo'ker	ביוקר
insurance	bitu'akh	ביטוח
cancellation	bitul'	ביטול
recreation	biluy'	בילוי
have a nice time	bilu'y naim'	בילוי נעים
between, among	beyn	בין
among other	beyn hasha'ar	בין השאר
in any case	beyn ko vakho'	בין כה וכה
intercity	beyn"ironi'	בינעירוני
meanwhile	beinta'yim	בינתיים
egg	beytsa'	ביצה
performance	bitsua'	ביצוע
visit (n.)	bikur'	ביקור
control, criticism	biko'ret	ביקורת
passport control	biko'ret darkonim'	ביקורת דרכונים
beer	bi'ra	בירה
malt beer	bi'ra shkhora'	בירה שחורה
clarification, consideration	birur'	בירור
cooking	bishul'	בישול
home, house	bayt	בית

hospital	beyt kholim'	בית חולים
prison	beyt ke'le	בית כלא
Bethlehem	beyt le'khem	בית לחם
court	beyt mishpat'	בית משפט
school	beyt se'fer	בית ספר
cottage	bayt katan'	בית קטן
coffeeshop, coffeehouse	beyt kafe'	בית קפה
on purpose, purposely	bekhavana'	בכוונה
potentially; by force	bako'akh	בכח
crying	be'khi	בכי
in all the details	bekhol' hapratim'	בכל הפרטים
seriously	bekhol' hartsinut'	בכל הרצינות
nevertheless	bekhol' zot	בכל זאת
altogether, in general	bikhlal'	בכלל
not at all	bikhlal' lo	בכלל לא
honestly	bekhenut'	בכנות
without	belo'	בלא
unintentionally	belo' kavana'	בלא כוונה
no smoking section	belo' meashnim'	בלא מעשנים
mix up, confusion	bilbul'	בלבול
mess	balagan'	בלגן
anyway	belav' hakhi'	בלוא הכי
without	bli	בלי
mindlessly	bli rosh	בלי ראש
not having a choice	beleyt' brera'	בלית ברירה
brakes	blamim'	בלמים
mockingly	bela'ag	בלעג
not	bil'ti	בלתי
precisely	bimeduyak'	במדויק
on Saturday evening	bemotsey' shabat'	במוצאי שבת
especially	bimyukhad'	במיוחד
parallel to	bemakbil'	במקביל
instead of	bimkom'	במקום
by chance	bemikre'	במקרה
in the distance	bemerkhak'	במרחק
vigorously	beme'rets	במרץ
during	beme'shekh	במשך
during the trip	beme'shekh hanesia'	במשך הנסיעה
purposely	bemitkaven'	במתכוון
son	ben	בן
son of a bitch	ben zona'	בן זונה
concerning	benoge'a le	בנוגע ל־
concerning which	benoge'a lekhakh'	בנוגע לכך
building, construction	binyan'	בנין
banana(s)	bana'na (bana'not)	בננה (בננות)
separately	benifrad'	בנפרד
bank	bank	בנק
o.k.	bese'der	בסדר

perfectly all right, perfectly fine, o.k.	bese'der gamur'	בסדר גמור
finally, at the end	besof'	בסוף
ultimately	besofo' shel davar'	בסופו של דבר
base	basis'	בסיס
biscuit	biskvit'	בסקוויט
through, for	bead'	בעד
for him	beado'	בעדו
while	beod'	בעוד
in a while	beod' zman ma	בעוד זמן מה
God willing!	beezrat' hashem'	בעזרת השם
problem	baya'	בעיה
mainly, especially	beikar'	בעיקר
husband	baal'	בעל
my husband	baali'	בעלי
owner (owners)	baalim'	בעלים
actually	bae'tsem	בעצם
indirectly	beakifin'	בעקיפין
in the evening	bae'rev	בערב
on Friday evening	bee'rev shabat'	בערב שבת
publicly	befumbey'	בפומבי
impulsively	bifzizut'	בפזיזות
inside	bifnim'	בפנים
explicitly	beferush'	בפרוש
absolutely not	beferush' lo	בפרוש לא
justly, rightly so	betse'dek	בצדק
grape harvest	batsir'	בציר
onion	batsal'	בצל
dough	batsek'	בצק
bottle	bakbuk'	בקבוק
hardly	beko'shi	בקושי
in short	bekitsur'	בקיצור
soon	bekarov'	בקרוב
request (n.)	bakasha'	בקשה
lucky person	bar mazal'	בר מזל
first and foremost	berosh' varishona'	בראש וראשונה
at first	berishona'	בראשונה
duck (n.)	barvaz'	ברווז
welcome!	barukh' haba'!	ברוך הבא!
thank God!	barukh' hashem'!	ברוך השם!
barometer	barome'ter	ברומטר
clearly	barur'	ברור
undoubtedly	barur' meal' lekhol' safek'	ברור מעל לכל ספק
iron	barzel'	ברזל
healthy	bari'	בריא
bolt (n.)	bari'yakh	בריח
escape (n.)	brikha'	בריחה
swimming pool	brekha'	בריכה
alliance	brit	ברית

knee	be'rekh	ברך
lap, knees	birka'im	ברכיים
hintingly	bere'mez	ברמז
brandy	bren'di	ברנדי
character	barnash'	ברנש
gladly	beratson'	ברצון
next week	beshavu'a haba'	בשבוע הבא
in order to	bishvil	בשביל
definitely not!	beshum' panim' vao'fen!	בשום פנים ואופן!
ripe	bashel'	בשל
quietly	beshe'ket	בשקט
meat	basar'	בשר
meat (kashrut)	basari'	בשרי
silently	bishtika'	בשתיקה
daughter	bat	בת
understandingly	bitvuna'	בתבונה
within	betokh'	בתוך
valid	beto'kef	בתוקף
on line	betor'	בתור
on condition that	betnay' she...	בתנאי ש...

ג

proud	gee'	גאה
pride	gaava'	גאווה
high tide	geut'	גאות
jeans	jins	ג'ינס
back	gav	גב
high	gavo'a	גבוה
tall	gavo'a	גבוה
limit, boundary	gvul	גבול
white cheese	gvina' levana'	גבינה לבנה
yellow cheese	gvina' tsehuba'	גבינה צהובה
cheeses	gvinot'	גבינות
hill	giv"a'	גבעה
man	ge'ver	גבר
lady	gve'ret	גברת
big, large	gadol'	גדול
fence	gader'	גדר
height	go'va	גובה
size, magnitude	go'del	גודל
shade	gavan'	גוון
goal (football)	gol	גול
zombie	go'lem	גולם
raw	golmi'	גולמי
golf	golf	גולף
rubber	gu'mi	גומי
finishes	gomer'	גומר
body	guf	גוף

undershirt	gufiya'	גופיה
gas	gaz	גז
carrot	ge'zer	גזר
valley	gi	גיא
geography	geogra'fia	גיאוגרפיה
age	gil	גיל
finish (n.)	gimur'	גימור
garden	gina'	גינה
chalk	gir	גיר
deportation of refugees	geru'sh plitim'	גירוש פליטים
divorce (n.)	gerushin'	גירושין
wave (n.)	gal	גל
open (adj.)(m.)	galuy'	גלוי
open (adj.)(f.)	gluya'	גלויה
postcard	gluya'	גלויה
ice cream	gli'da	גלידה
Galilee	galil'	גליל
too, also	gam	גם
also	gam, gam ken	גם, גם כן
dwarf	gamad'	גמד
camel	gamal'	גמל
finish (n.)	gmar	גמר
park (n.)	gan	גן
zoo	gan khayot'	גן חיות
kindergarten	gan yeladim'	גן ילדים
pejorative	gnay	גנאי
thief (m.)	ganav'	גנב
thief (f.)	ganev'et	גנבת
theft	gniva'	גניבה
kindergarten teacher	gane'net	גננת
coarse	gas	גס
limbs	gapa'im	גפיים
vine	ge'fen	גפן
convert (n.)	ger	גר
socks	garba'im	גרביים
throat	garon'	גרון
horrible	garu'a	גרוע
ax	garzen'	גרזן
grease (n.)	griz	גריז
barley	grisim'	גריסים
nucleus	gar"in'	גרעין
sunflower seeds	gar"inim'	גרעינים
rainy	gashum'	גשום
rain (n.)	ge'shem	גשם

ד

worry (n.)	daaga'	דאגה
bee	dvora'	דבורה

glue	de'vek	דבק
speak up!	daber'!	דבר!
something	davar'	דבר
milk products	divrey' khalav'	דברי חלב
honey	dvash	דבש
fish (fish)	dag (dagim')	דג (דגים)
pickled fish	dag malu'akh	דג מלוח
smoked fish	dag meushan'	דג מעושן
saltwater fish	dagey' yam	דגי ים
flag	de'gel	דגל
Post, post office	do'ar	דואר
bear (n.)	dov	דוב
spokesperson	dover'	דובר
uncle	dod	דוד
report (n.)	du'akh	דוח
aunt	do'da	דודה
pedal	davsha'	דוושה
accelerator	davshat' gaz	דוושת גז
dollar	do'lar	דולר
generation	dor	דור
demand (v.)	doresh'	דורש
urgent	dakhuf'	דחוף
rejection	dkhiya'	דחיה
compression	dkhisa'	דחיסה
push (n.)	dkhifa'	דחיפה
impulse	da'khaf	דחף
diet	die'ta	דיאטה
ink	d"yo	דיו
stewardess	daye'let	דיילת
discotheque	diskotek'	דיסקוטק
apartment	dira'	דירה
gasoline, fuel, petrol	de'lek	דלק
door	de'let	דלת
December	detsem'ber	דצמבר
thin	dak	דק
minute (n.)	daka'	דקה
south	darom'	דרום
demand (n.)	drisha'	דרישה
regards	drishat' shalom'	דרישת שלום
route, way	de'rekh	דרך
passport	darkon'	דרכון
grass	de'she	דשא
religion	dat	דת
religious (m.)	dati'	דתי
religious (f.)	datiya'	דתיה

ה

recent	haakharon'	האחרון
isn't it true?	haeyn' ze nakhon'?	האין זה נכון?

this man	haish' haze'	האיש הזה
do you?	haim'?	האם?
does it?	haim'?	האם?
next	haba'	הבא
let's, come on	ha'va	הבה
promise	havtakha'	הבטחה
the house	haba'yt	הבית
home	habay'ta	הביתה
magnification	hagdala'	הגדלה
definition	hagdara'	הגדרה
steering wheel	he'ge	הגה
migration	hagira'	הגירה
defense, protection	hagana'	הגנה
echo	hed	הד
this thing	hadavar' haze'	הדבר הזה
these things	hadvarim' haey'lu	הדברים האלו
refund	hekhzer'	החזר
he	hu	הוא
admission, thanks	hodaa'	הודאה
turkey	ho'du	הודו
message	hodaa'	הודעה
go (m.)(f.) (present)	holekh', hole'khet	הולך, הולכת
conduction	holakha'	הולכה
capital	hon	הון
fraud, deceit	honaa'	הונאה
decrease, unloading	horada'	הורדה
order (n.)	hazmana'	הזמנה
special invitation	hazmana' meyukhe'det	הזמנה מיוחדת
reflection	hakhzara'	החזרה
resolution, decision	hakhlata'	החלטה
recovery	hakhlama'	החלמה
best	hatov' beyoter'	הטוב ביותר
she	hi	היא
was, it was (m.)	haya'	היה
today	hayom'	היום
being that	heyot' ve...	היות ו...
was (f.)	hayta'	היתה
the Western Wall	hako'tel	הכותל
everything	hakol'	הכל
everything is fine	hakol' bese'der	הכל בסדר
recognition	hakara'	הכרה
farther	ha'l"a	הלאה
loan (n.)	halvaa'	הלוואה
may it be	halevay'	הלוואי
solder	halkhama'	הלחמה
they (m.)	hem	הם
large number	hamon'	המון
they (f.)	hen	הן
engineering	handasa'	הנדסה
explanation	hesber'	הסבר

quarantine	hesger'	הסגר
arrangement	hesder'	הסדר
history	histo'ria	הסטוריה
agreement	haskama'	הסכמה
escalation	haslama'	הסלמה
ride, transportation	hasaa'	הסעה
eulogy	hesped'	הספד
heating	hasaka'	הסקה
main thing	haikar'	העיקר
to town	hai'ra	העירה
rise (n.), increase	haalaa'	העלאה
demonstration	hafgana'	הפגנה
pause (n.)	hafuga'	הפוגה
voyage (n.)	haflaga'	הפלגה
abortion, miscarriage	hapala'	הפלה
break, intermission	hafsaka'	הפסקה
bombing	haftsatsa'	הפצצה
deposit (money)	hafkada'	הפקדה
production	hafaka'	הפקה
nullification	hafara'	הפרה
vote (n.)	hatsbaa'	הצבעה
play, show (n.)	hatsaga'	הצגה
success	hatslakha'	הצלחה
relief, easing	hakala'	הקלה
mountain	har	הר
the Temple Mount	har haba'it	הר הבית
a lot, many, much	harbe'	הרבה
habit	hergel'	הרגל
feeling	hargasha'	הרגשה
lousy feeling	hargasha' mezupe'tet	הרגשה מזופטת
wonderful feeling	hargasha' metsuye'net	הרגשה מצוינת
anesthesia	hardama'	הרדמה
behold	harey'	הרי
adventure	harpatka'	הרפתקה
allow me	harshe' li	הרשה לי
impact (n.)	hashpaa'	השפעה
irrigation	hashkaya'	השקיה
investment	hashkaa'	השקעה
inspiration	hashraa'	השראה
suicide	hit"abdut'	התאבדות
assimilation	hitbolelut'	התבוללות
duty	hitkhayvut'	התחייבות
contraction	hitkavtsut'	התכווצות
correspondence	hitkatvut'	התכתבות
embitterment	hitmarmerut'	התמרמרות
resistance	hitnagdut'	התנגדות
behavior	hitnahagut'	התנהגות
starting (machine)	hatnaa'	התנעה
gym, exercise	hit"amlut'	התעמלות
expansion	hitpashtut'	התפשטות

progress (n.)	hitkadmut'	התקדמות
attack (n.)	hatkafa'	התקפה
excitement	hitragshut'	התרגשות
contribution	hatrama'	התרמה

ו

and	ve...	...ו
and even so	uvekhol' zot	ובכל זאת
and so	uvekhen'	ובכן
hook	vav	וו
certain	vadai'	וודאי
certainly	vaday'	וודאי
vodka	vod'ka	וודקה
video	vi'deo	ווידאו
visa	vi'za	ויזה
vitamin (vitamins)	vitamin' (vitamin'im)	ויטמין (ויטמינים)
curtain	vilon'	וילון
indicator lights	vin'kerim	וינקרים
virus	vi'rus	וירוס
windshield wiper	vi'sher	וישר
and what of it?	uma' bekhakh'?	ומה בכך?
rose	ve'red	ורד
pink	varod'	ורוד
and that's it!	vetu' lo!	ותו לא!
seniority	ve'tek	ותק

ז

jacket	jaket'	ז'קט
wolf	zeev'	זאב
that means, that is to say	zot ome'ret	זאת אומרת
this (f.)	zot, zo	זאת, זו
fly (flies)	zvuv (zvuvim')	זבוב, זבובים
it, this (m.),	ze	זה
It is, this is a/an	ze	זה
that is because	ze biglal' she...	זה בגלל ש...
this is for	ze bishvil'	זה בשביל
that's good	ze tov	זה טוב
that's foolish	ze tipshi'	זה טפשי
that's nice	ze yafe'	זה יפה
it's expensive	ze yakar'	זה יקר
I don't care	ze lo meziz' li	זה לא מזיז לי
that's not enough	ze lo maspik'	זה לא מספיק
that it isn't so	ze lo nakhon'	זה לא נכון
long ago	ze mikvar'	זה מכבר
that's enough	ze maspik'	זה מספיק
that's boring	ze meshaamem'	זה משעמם
does it open?	ze niftakh'?	זה נפתח?

it costs	ze ole	זה עולה
it depends	ze talu'y	זה תלוי
gold	zahav'	זהב
that's it	ze'hu ze	זהו זה
careful (m.)	zahir'	זהיר
careful (f.)	zhira'	זהירה
this (f.)	zo, zo'hi	זו, זוהי
horrible	zvaa'	זוועה
minor, junior	zutar'	זוטר
angle	zavit'	זווית
cheap, inexpensive	zol	זול
fellow man	zulat'	זולת
except for	zulat'	זולת
prostitute	zona'	זונה
let's go?	zaz'nu?	זזנו?
infection	zihum'	זיהום
olive (olives)	za'it (zeitim')	זית (זיתים)
human rights	zkhuyot' adam'	זכויות אדם
glass	zkhukhit'	זכוכית
male	zakhar'	זכר
memory	zikaron'	זכרון
of blessed memory	zal	ז"ל
available	zamin'	זמין
time	zman	זמן
temporary	zmani'	זמני
hard times	zmanim' kashim'	זמנים קשים
singer (m.)	zamar'	זמר
singer (f.)	zame'ret	זמרת
erect (adj.)	zakuf'	זקוף
old (age) (m.)	zaken'	זקן
old (age) (f.)	zkena'	זקנה
foreign	zar	זר
quick	zariz'	זריז
sunrise	zrikhat' she'mesh	זריחת שמש
current	ze'rem	זרם
electric current	ze'rem khashmali'	זרם חשמלי
direct current	ze'rem kavu'a	זרם קבוע

ח

likable (m.)	khaviv'	חביב
likable (f.)	khaviva'	חביבה
fried egg	khavita'	חביתה
rope	khe'vel	חבל
pity	khaval'	חבל
member	khaver'	חבר
friend (m.) (friends)	khaver' (khaverim')	חבר (חברים)
friend (f.)	khavera'	חברה
society	khevra'	חברה
Knesset members	khavrey' kne'set	חברי כנסת

holiday	khag	חג
belt	khagura'	חגורה
seat belt	khagurat' betikhut'	חגורת בטיחות
sharp	khad	חד
smoothly	khad vekhalak'	חד וחלק
monotonous	khadgoni'	חדגוני
permeable	khadir'	חדיר
penetration	khadira'	חדירה
room	khe'der	חדר
emergency room	khadar' miyun'	חדר מיון
bedroom	khadar' shena'	חדר שינה
new (m.)	khadash'	חדש
new (f.)	khadasha'	חדשה
news	khadashot'	חדשות
month	kho'desh	חודש
contract	khoze'	חוזה
peace agreement	khoze' shalom'	חוזה שלום
rope, string	khut	חוט
abroad	khul	חו"ל
sand	khol	חול
sick (m.)	khole'	חולה
sick (f.)	khola'	חולה
shirt	khultsa'	חולצה
temperature	khom	חום
brown	khum'	חום
wall	khoma'	חומה
vinegar	kho'metz	חומץ
acid	khumtsa'	חומצה
material	kho'mer	חומר
raw material	kho'mer ge'lem	חומר גלם
lack of	kho'ser	חוסר
irresponsibility	kho'ser akhrayut'	חוסר אחראיות
coast, shore	khof'	חוף
beach, seashore	khof hayam'	חוף הים
wedding canopy	khupa'	חופה
freedom	kho'fesh	חופש
vacation	khufsha'	חופשה
nice vacation	khufsha' neima'	חופשה נעימה
outside	khuts	חוץ
except for	khuts mi...	חוץ מ...
except for me	khuts mime'ni	חוץ ממני
nervy	khutspan', khutspanit'	חוצפן, חוצפנית
law	khok	חוק
legal	khuki'	חוקי
researcher	khoker'	חוקר
hole	khor	חור
winter	kho'ref	חורף
grove	kho'resh	חורש
sense (n.)	khush	חוש
dark	kho'shekh	חושך

total darkness	kho'shekh mitsra'yim	חושך מצריים
chest	khaze'	חזה
pig!	khazir'!	חזיר!
front	khazit'	חזית
strong	khazak'	חזק
return, review, rehearsal	khazara'	חזרה
alive	khay	חי
connection	khibur'	חיבור
animal	khaya'	חיה
positivity; debiting	khiyuv'	חיוב
positive	khiyuvi'	חיובי
smile (n.)	khiyukh'	חיוך
vital	khiyuni'	חיוני
owes, must (m.)	khayav'	חייב
owes, must (f.)	khayev'et	חייבת
soldier (m.)	khayal'	חייל
soldier (f.)	khaye'let	חיילת
soldiers	khayalim'	חיילים
life	khaim'	חיים
non-religious (m.)	khiloni'	חילוני
non-religious (f.)	khilonit'	חילונית
education	khinukh'	חינוך
free (adv.)	khinam'	חינם
search (n.)	khipusim'	חיפושים
external (adj.)(m.)	khitsoni'	חיצוני
freedom	kherut'	חירות
calculation	khishuv'	חישוב
wait a minute!	khake' re'ga!	חכה רגע!
wise, intelligent (m.)	khakham'	חכם
milk	khalav'	חלב
dairy	khalavi'	חלבי
dream	khalom'	חלום
sweet dreams	khalomot' metukim'	חלומות מתוקים
window	khalon'	חלון
robe	khaluk'	חלוק
distribution	khaluka'	חלוקה
back part	khe'lek akhori'	חלק אחורי
smooth	khalak'	חלק
top	khe'lek el"yon'	חלק עליון
slight	khalash'	חלש
weak (m.)	khalash'	חלש
weak (f.)	khalasha'	חלשה
hot, warm (m.)	kham	חם
hot, warm (f.)	khama'	חמה
butter	khem"a'	חמאה
cute (m.)	khamud'	חמוד
cute (f.)	khamuda'	חמודה
sour (m.)	khamuts'	חמוץ
sour (f.)	khamutsa'	חמוצה

donkey	khamor'	חמור
grave (adj.)	khamur'	חמור
five	khamisha'	חמישה
fifteen	khamisha' asar'	חמישה עשר
fifth	khamishi'	חמישי
fifty	khamishim'	חמישים
hot desert wind	khamsin'	חמסין
clay	khemar'	חמר
shop, store	khanut'	חנות
bookstore	khanut' sfarim'	חנות ספרים
parking	khanaya'	חניה
paid parking	khanaya' betashlum'	חניה בתשלום
God forbid!	khas veshalom'!	חס ושלום!
blockage	khasima'	חסימה
immunity	khasinut'	חסינות
absent	khaser'	חסר
absence	khisaron'	חסרון
innocent	khaf mipe'sha	חף מפשע
superficially	khafif'	חפיף
excavation	khafira'	חפירה
arrow	khets	חץ
skirt	khatsait'	חצאית
midnight	khatsot'	חצות
half	khetsi'	חצי
half a kilogram	khatsi' ki'lo	חצי קילו
eggplant	khatsilim'	חצילים
yard	khatser'	חצר
gravel	khatsats'	חצץ
investigation	khakira'	חקירה
ultraorthodox	kharedi'	חרדי
mustard	khardal'	חרדל
bead (beads)	kharuz' (kharuzim)'	חרוז (חרוזים)
irregular	kharig'	חריג
spicy	kharif'	חריף
insects	kharakim'	חרקים
math, bill, account	kheshbon'	חשבון
arithmetic	kheshbon'	חשבון
important	khashuv'	חשוב
importance	khashivut'	חשיבות
electricity	khashmal'	חשמל
electrician	khashmalay'	חשמלאי
electric, electrical	khashmali'	חשמלי
is cut	khatukh'	חתוך
cat (cats)	khatul' (khatulim')	חתול (חתולים)
handsome, cute	khatikh'	חתיך
beautiful, a piece	khatikha'	חתיכה
cut (n.)	khatakh'	חתך

ט

cook (m.)	tabakh'	טבח
cook (f.)	tabakhit'	טבחית
cook (v.)	levashel'	לבשל
nature	te'va	טבע
natural	tiv"i', tiv"it'	טבעי, טבעית
well, good	tov	טוב
well and good	tov veyafe'	טוב ויפה
very good	tov meod'	טוב מאוד
good (f.)	tova'	טובה
favor (n.)	tova'	טובה
idiot	tum'tum	טומטום
toast (n.)	tost	טוסט
form	to'fes	טופס
hike, trip, sightseeing, excursion	tiyul'	טיול
plaster	ti'yakh	טיח
pilot	tayas'	טיס
flight	tisa'	טיסה
flight departures	tisot' yots"ot'	טיסות יוצאות
bit	tipa'	טיפה
fool (n.)	tipesh'	טיפש
technician	tekhnai'	טכנאי
dew	tal	טל
television, TV	televi'ziya	טלוויזיה
telephone	telefon'	טלפון
tennis	te'nis	טניס
ping pong	te'nis shulkhan'	טניס שולחן
inspection test (for car)	test	טסט
mistake (n.)	taut'	טעות
tasty (m.)	taim'	טעים
tasty (f.)	teima'	טעימה
taste (n.)	ta'am	טעם
fresh (m.)	tari'	טרי
fresh (f.)	triya'	טריה
not yet	te'rem	טרם
tractor	tra'ktor	טרקטור

י

enter! come in!	yavo'!	יבוא!
blister (n.)	yabe'let	יבלת
dry (adj.)	yavesh'	יבש
hand (hands)	yad (yada'im)	יד (ידיים)
knowledge	yedia'	ידיע
good news	yedia' mesama'khat	ידיעה משמחת
there will be	yihye'	יהיה
it'll be o.k.	yihye' bese'der	יהיה בסדר
diamond	yahalom'	יהלום

woman giving birth	yole'det	יולדת
July	yu'li	יולי
day	yom	יום
birthday	yom hule'det	יום הולדת
two days	yoma'im	יומיים
June	yu'ni	יוני
July	yu'li	יולי
beauty	yo'fi	יופי
more	yoter'	יותר
too much	yoter' miday'	יותר מדי
more than this	yoter' mize'	יותר מזה
more than anything	yoter' mikol'	יותר מכל
together	ya'khad	יחד
single	yakhid'	יחיד
relation	ya'khas	יחס
wine	ya'in	יין
white wine	ya'in lavan'	יין לבן
red wine	ya'in adom'	יין אדום
production	yetsur'	ייצור
can	yakhol'	יכול
could be	yakhol' lih"yot'	יכול להיות
ability, capability	yakho'let	יכולת
boy	ye'led	ילד
children	yeladim'	ילדים
sea	yam	ים
Dead Sea	yam hame'lakh	ים המלח
Red Sea	yam suf	ים סוף
right	yamin'	ימין
to the right	yami'na	ימינה
January	ya'nuar	ינואר
arm (n.)	yad	יד
handle (n.)	yadit'	ידית
efficiency	ya"ilut'	יעילות
good-looking (m.)	yafe'	יפה
good-looking (f.)	yafa'	יפה
nice	yafe'	יפה
export	yetsu'	יצוא
exit	yetsia'	יציאה
emergency exit	yetsiat' kherum'	יציאת חרום
producer	yatsran'	יצרן
vineyard	ye'kev	יקב
precious	yakar'	יקר
Jordan	yarden'	ירדן
green (m.)	yarok'	ירוק
green (f.)	yeruka'	ירוקה
inheritance	yerusha'	ירושה
Jerusalem	yerushala'im	ירושלים
exposition	yarid'	יריד
book fair	yerid' sfarim'	יריד ספרים
decline, emigration	yerida'	ירידה

vegetables	yerakot'	ירקות
grocery	yarkan'	ירקן
greenish	yarakrak'	ירקרק
have, here is, there is/are	yesh	יש
there are all kinds	yesh vayesh'	יש ויש
rear end	yashvan'	ישבן
settlement	yeshuv'	ישוב
implementation	yisum'	ישום
seating	yeshiva'	ישיבה
direct (adj.)	yashir'	ישיר
old (m.)	yashan'	ישן
old (f.)	yeshana'	ישנה
straight	yashar'	ישר
mosquito (mosquitoes)	yetush (yetushim')	יתוש (יתושים)
moreover	yetira' mikakh'	יתירה מכך
it is possible	yitakhen'	יתכן
moreover	ye'ter al ken	יתר על כן

כ

personnel department	ko'akh adam'	כ"א (כוח אדם)
pain (n.)	keev'	כאב
headache	keev' rosh	כאב ראש
as if	kei'lu	כאילו
here	kan	כאן
liver	kaved'	כבד
heavy	kaved'	כבד
seemingly	kivyakhol'	כביכול
laundry	kvisa'	כביסה
road	kvish	כביש
cable	ke'vel	כבל
already	kvar	כבר
it's too late	kvar meukhar'	כבר מאוחר
right now	kvar akhshav'	כבר עכשיו
sheep	ke'ves	כבש
it's worthwhile	keday'	כדאי
let's hurry	keday' lehizdarez'	כדאי להזדרז
ball	kadur'	כדור
	kaduryad'	כדור יד
football	kadure'gel amerika'i	כדורגל אמריקאי
soccer	kadure'gel	כדורגל
basketball	kadursal'	כדורסל
hat, cap	ko'va	כובע
personnel	koach' adam'	כוח אדם
burn (n.)	kviya'	כויה
star (n.)	kokhav'	כוכב
any	kol	כול

anyone	kol ekhad'	כול אחד
anything	kol davar'	כול דבר
total	kolel'	כולל
everybody	kulam'	כולם
cap (army)	kumta'	כומתה
(on) alert	konenut'	כוננות
bookcase	konenit' sfarim'	כוננית ספרים
cup	kos	כוס
small cup	kosit'	כוסית
armchair(s)	kursa'	כורסא
cotton	kutna'	כותנה
like this (m.)	kaze'	כזה
like this (f.)	kazot'	כזאת
the type that	kaze' she...	כזה ש...
power	ko'akh	כח
blue	kakhol'	כחול
direction	kivun'	כיוון
because	keyvan' she...	כיוון ש...
sink (n.)	kiyor'	כיור
chemist	kimai'	כימאי
chemistry	ki'miya	כימיה
assembly	kinus'	כינוס
pocket	kis	כיס
cover (n.)	kisu'y	כיסוי
bedcover	kisu'y lemita'	כיסוי למיטה
head covering	kisuy' rosh	כיסוי ראש
fun	keyf	כיף
surgery	kirurgi'a	כירורגיה
magic	kishuf'	כישוף
class, classroom	kita'	כיתה
this way, thus	kakh	כך
so	ka'kha	ככה
so-so	ka'kha ka'kha	ככה ככה
all, every	kol	כל
everyone, each	kol ekhad'	כל אחד
all the way	kol hade'rekh	כל הדרך
all the time	kol hazman'	כל הזמן
congratulations	kol hakavod'	כל הכבוד
good luck, best wishes	kol tuv lekha'	כל טוב לך
all day	kol yom'	כל יום
so	kol kakh	כל כך
so beautiful	kol kakh' yafe'	כל כך יפה
every night	kol lay'la	כל לילה
as long as	kol od	כל עוד
dog	ke'lev	כלב
nothing	klum	כלום
tool	kli	כלי
weapon	kley ne'shek	כלי נשק
tools	kelim'	כלים
economy	kalkala'	כלכלה

how much, how many	ka'ma	כמה
quite a few years	ka'ma shanim' tovot'	כמה שנים טובות
like (adv.)	kmo	כמו
like nothing	kmo klum	כמו כלום
certainly; of course	kamuvan'	כמובן
quantity	kamut'	כמות
certain amount	kamut' mesuye'met	כמות מסויימת
yes	ken	כן
honest, frank	ken	כן
yes, of course	ken, kamuvan'	כן, כמובן
entry, entrance	knisa'	כניסה
personnel only	knisa' betafkid'	כניסה בתפקיד
yield	knia'	כניעה
fine	knas	כנס
the Church of the Holy Sepulchre	knesiyat' hake'ver	כנסיית הקבר
Knesset	kne'set	כנסת
chair (chairs)	kise' (kisaot')	כסא (כסאות)
money	ke'sef	כסף
anger (n.)	ka'as	כעס
spoon (spoons)	kaf (kapot')	כף (כפות)
tablespoon	kaf	כף
double	kaful'	כפול
apparently	kfi hanir"e'	כפי הנראה
as	kfi	כפי
as you know	kfi sheata' yode'a	כפי שאתה יודע
as needed	kfi shetsarikh'	כפי שצריך
teaspoon	kapit'	כפית
glove	kfafa'	כפפה
village	kfar	כפר
cabbage	kruv	כרוב
ticket, card	kartis'	כרטיס
pillow	karit'	כרית
correspondent	katav'	כתב
handwriting	ktav yad	כתב יד
journal	ktav"et'	כתב־עת
article (news)	katava'	כתבה
is written	katuv'	כתוב
address (n.)	kto'vet	כתובת
orange	katom'	כתום

ל

no, not	lo	לא
not the same thing	lo oto' davar'	לא אותו דבר
nobody cares	lo' ikhpat'	לא איכפת
	leaf ekhad'	לאף אחד
no way!	lo ba bekheshbon'!	לא בא בחשבון!
not exactly	lo bediyuk'	לא בדיוק
not certain	lo batu'akh	לא בטוח

not in order to	lo bikhdi'	לא בכדי
not everything	lo hakol'	לא הכל
not a lot	lo harbe'	לא הרבה
not that!	lo ze!	לא זה!
not good	lo tov	לא טוב
I didn't know	lo yada'ti	לא ידעתי
unable	lo yakhol'	לא יכול
it can't be	lo yakhol' lih"yot'	לא יכול להיות
it is not possible	lo yitakhen'	לא יתכן
not worthwhile	lo keday'	לא כדאי
not this way	lo ka'kha	לא ככה
not so much, not so good	lo kol kakh'	לא כל כך
inaccurate	lo meduyak'	לא מדויק
recently, not long ago	lo mizman'	לא מזמן
not significant	lo mashmauti'	לא משמעותי
unsuitable	lo mat"im'	לא מתאים
uncomfortable	lo nu'akh	לא נוח
wrong, incorrect, incorrectly	lo nakhon'	לא נכון
away	lo nimtsa'	לא נמצא
unpleasant	lo naim'	לא נעים
nothing remains	lo nish"ar' klum	לא נשאר כלום
don't bother	lo tsarikh'	לא צריך
not connected, related	lo kashur'	לא קשור
I don't want to!	lo rotse'!	לא רוצה!
not there	lo sham	לא שם
not useful	lo shimushi'	לא שמושי
love (v.)	leehov'	לאהוב
not really! not necessarily	lav dav'ka	לאו דווקא
nationality	leom'	לאום
national	leumi'	לאומי
nationalism	leumanut'	לאומנות
as opposed to	leumat'	לאומת
in light of	leor'	לאור
unite (v.)	leakhed'	לאחד
be late	leakher'	לאחר
after	leakhar'	לאחר
slowly	leat'	לאט
eat	leekhol'	לאכול
to where?	lean'?	לאן?
gather	leesof'	לאסוף
bake	leefot'	לאפות
confirm	le"asher'	לאשר
heart	lev	לב
alone	levad'	לבד

check (v.), examine (v.)	livdok'	לבדוק
come	lavo'	לבוא
choose (v.)	livkhor'	לבחור
trust (v.)	livto'akh	לבטוח
cancel	levatel'	לבטל
cry (v.)	livkot'	לבכות
spend time	levalot'	לבלות
white	lavan'	לבן
build	livnot'	לבנות
underwear	levanim'	לבנים
kick (v.)	liv"ot'	לבעוט
implement (v.)	levatse'a	לבצע
visit (v.)	levaker'	לבקר
request (v.), ask for	levakesh'	לבקש
find out	levarer'	לברר
cook (v.)	levashel'	לבשל
about	legabey'	לגבי
grow	ligdol'	לגדול
live (v.)	lagur'	לגור
finish (v.)	ligmor'	לגמור
entirely, completely	legam'rey	לגמרי
touch (v.)	laga'at	לגעת
cause (v.)	ligrom'	לגרום
speak	ledaber'	לדבר
report (v.)	ledave'yakh	לדווח
know	lada'at	לדעת
believe	lehaamin'	להאמין
flame	lehava'	להבה
clarify, make clear	lehav"hir'	להבהיר
bring	lehavi'	להביא
realize (v.), understand (v.)	lehavin'	להבין
recover	lehavri'	להבריא
shine (v.)	lehavrik'	להבריק
say, tell	lehagid'	להגיד
reach, arrive	lehagi'a	להגיע
protect	lehagen'	להגן
that's a lie	lehadam'	להד"מ
print (v.)	lehadpis'	להדפיס
thank (v.)	lehodot'	להודות
prove (v.)	lehokhi'yakh	להוכיח
announce (v.)	lehodi'a	להודיע
add (v.)	lehosif'	להוסיף
take out	lehotsi'	להוציא
spend	lehotsi' ke'sef	להוציא כסף
happen	lehizdamen'	להזדמן
be careful	lehizaher'	להזהר
hold	lehakhzik'	להחזיק
return, refund	lehakhzir'	להחזיר

be	lih"yot'	להיות
to become a(n)	lihyot' le...	להיות ל...
enter (v.)	lehikanes'	להיכנס
disappear	lehialem'	להיעלם
prepare	lehakhin'	להכין
admit	lehakhnis'	להכניס
dictate	lehakhtiv'	להכתיב
recommend	lehamlits'	להמליץ
continue	lehamshikh'	להמשיך
suppose	lehani'yakh	להניח
explain	lehasbir'	להסביר
get	lehasig'	להסיג
agree	lehaskim'	להסכים
approve	lehaskim' le...	להסכים ל...
turn around	lehistovev'	להסתובב
prefer	lehaadif'	להעדיף
evaluate	lehaarikh'	להעריך
admire	lehaarits'	להעריץ
meet	lehipagesh'	להפגש
join	lehitstaref'	להצטרף
show (v.)	lehatsig'	להציג
propose	lehatsi'a	להציע
succeed in	lehatsli'yakh be...	להצליח ב...
reduce	lehaktin'	להקטין
freeze	lehakpi'	להקפיא
feel	lehargish'	להרגיש
destroy	leharos'	להרוס
raise (v.)	leharim'	להרים
allow	leharshot'	להרשות
boil (v.)	leharti'yakh	להרתיח
stay (v.)	lehishaer'	להשאר
reach (v.)	lehasig'	להשיג
invest (v.)	lehashki'a	להשקיע
mad, to go	lehishtage'a	להשתגע
participate	lehishtatef'	להשתתף
lie in the sun	lehishtazef'	להשתזף
hide (v.)	lehitkhabe'	להתחבא
begin, start	lehatkhil'	להתחיל
marry	lehitkhaten'	להתחתן
spray (v.)	lehatiz'	להתיז
refer	lehityakhes' el	להתיחס אל
wake up	lehit"orer'	להתעורר
pray	lehitpalel'	להתפלל
admire	lehitpael'	להתפעל
attack (v.)	lehatkif'	להתקיף
proceed	lehitkadem'	להתקדם
get in touch	lehitkasher'	להתקשר
see you! goodbye!	lehitraot'!	להתראות!
wash up	lehitrakhets'	להתרחץ
if not	lule'	לולא

English	Transliteration	Hebrew
say (v.)	lomar'	לומר
move (v.)	lazuz'	לזוז
damp	lakh	לח
high humidity	lakhut' gvoha'	לחות גבוהה
return, come back	lakhzor'...	לחזור...
go back	lakhzor' bekhazara'	לחזור בחזרה
return home	lakhzor' habay'ta	לחזור הביתה
repeat	lakhzor' al	לחזור על
live (v.)	likhyot'	לחיות
warfare	lekhima'	לחימה
dial (v.)	lekhayeg'	לחייג
bread	le'khem	לחם
look for	lekhapes'	לחפש
pressure (n.)	la'khats	לחץ
air pressure	la'khats avir'	לחץ אויר
high pressure	la'khats gavo'a	לחץ גבוה
think	lakhshov'	לחשוב
suspect (v.)	lakhshod'	לחשוד
fry (v.)	letagen'	לטגן
fly (v.)	latus'	לטוס
plaster (v.)	latayekh'	לטייח
travel, hike (v.)	letayel'	לטייל
phone (v.)	letalfen'	לטלפן
climb (v.)	letapes'	לטפס
to me	li	לי
near, next to	leyad'	ליד
enjoy	lehenot'	להנות
night	lay'la	לילה
good night	lay'la tov	לילה טוב
studying	limud'	לימוד
lemon	limon'	לימון
fall (v.)	lipol'	ליפול
shoot (v.)	lirot'	לירות
sleep (v.)	lishon'	לישון
wash (v.)	lekhabes'	לכבס
write	likhtov'	לכתוב
without	lelo'	ללא
useless	lelo' hoil'	ללא הועיל
unconscious	lelo' hakara'	ללא הכרה
non-stop	lelo' hefsek'	ללא הפסק
accompany	lelavot'	ללוות
go, walk	lale'khet	ללכת
teach	lelamed'	ללמד
study, learn	lilmod'	ללמוד
why?	la'ma?	למה?
for what	lema'	למה
die (v.)	lamut'	למות
below, down	lema'ta	למטה
sell (v.)	limkor'	למכור
prevent	limno'a	למנוע

excluding	lemaet’	למעט
up	lema’ala	למעלה
find (v.)	limtso’	למצוא
drive (v.)	linhog’	לנהוג
rest (v.)	lanu’akh	לנוח
guess (v.)	lenakhesh’	לנחש
travel (v.)	linso’a	לנסוע
try (v.)	lenasot’	לנסות
shake (v.)	lenaer’	לנער
kiss (v.)	lenashek’	לנשק
turn (v.)	lesovev’	לסובב
close (v.)	lisgor’	לסגור
arrange	lesader’	לסדר
forgive (v.)	lishlo’akh	לסלוח
indicate, mark (v.)	lesamen’	לסמן
dine	lis“od’	לסעוד
count (v.)	lispor’	לספור
refuse (v.)	lesarev’	לסרב
work (v.)	laavod’	לעבוד
cross (v.)	laavor’	לעבור
forever	leolam’	לעולם
leave (v.)	laazov’	לעזוב
help (v.)	laazor’	לעזור
sometimes	leitim’	לעיתים
often	leitim’ krovot’	לעיתים קרובות
seldom, rarely	leitim’ rekhokot’	לעיתים רחוקות
stand (v.)	laamod’	לעמוד
stop (v.)	laatsor’	לעצור
make, do	laasot’	לעשות
smoke (v.)	leashen’	לעשן
according to	lefi’	לפי
apply (v.)	lifnot’	לפנות
before, in front of	lifney’	לפני
before noon	lifney’ tsohora’im	לפני צהריים
previously	lifney’ khen	לפני כן
act (v.)	lif‘ol’	לפעול
sometimes	lif‘amim’	לפעמים
go out	latset’	לצאת
draw (v.)	letsayer’	לצייר
photograph (v.)	letsalem’	לצלם
accept, get, receive	lekabel’	לקבל
stand up	lakum’	לקום
take	laka’khat	לקחת
buy	liknot’	לקנות
leap, plunge (v.)	likpots’	לקפוץ
towards	likrat’	לקראת
read	likro’	לקרוא
call (v.)	likro’ le...	לקרוא ל...
see	lir“ot’	לראות
including	lerabot’	לרבות

chase (v.)	lirdof'	לרדוף
to a doctor	lerofe'	לרופא
run (v.)	laruts'	לרוץ
wash (v.)	lirkhots'	לרחוץ
want (v.)	lirtsot'	לרצות
dance (v.)	lirkod'	לרקוד
weld (v.)	leratekh'	לרתך
ask	lish"ol'	לשאול
sit	lashe'vet	לשבת
in vain	lashav'	לשווא
language, tongue	lashon'	לשון
sleep (v.)	lishon'	לישון
swim (v.)	liskhot'	לשחות
play (v.)	lesakhek'	לשחק
sing	lashir'	לשיר
lie, lie down	lishkav'	לשכב
rent (v.)	liskor'	לשכור
duplicate (v.)	leshakhpel'	לשכפל
send	lishlo'akh	לשלוח
pay (v.)	leshalem'	לשלם
be happy	lismo'akh	לשמוח
hear	lishmo'a	לשמוע
keep, store	lishmor'	לשמור
take care of	lishmor' al	לשמור על
change (v.)	leshanot'	לשנות
consider	lishkol'	לשקול
survive (v.)	lisrod'	לשרוד
be silent	lishtok'	לשתוק
drink (v.)	lishtot'	לשתות
share (v.)	leshatef'	לשתף
coordinate	letaem'	לתאם
describe	letaer'	לתאר
into	letokh'	לתוך
plan (v.)	letakhnen'	לתכנן
catch (v.)	litpos'	לתפוס
give (v.)	latet'	לתת

מ

fight (n.)	maavak'	מאבק
hundred	me'a	מאה
lover	meahev'	מאהב
very	meod'	מאוד
fan (n.)	meavrer'	מאוורר
late	meukhar'	מאוחר
disappointed (m.)	meukhzav'	מאוכזב
disappointed (f.)	meukhze'vet	מאוכזבת
vertical, perpendicular	meunakh'	מאונך
since	meaz'	מאז
scale	mozna'im	מאזניים

May	may	מאי
hundredth	meit'	מאית
coach (n.)	me'amen'	מאמן
article	maamar'	מאמר
arrest (n.)	maasar'	מאסר
bakery	maafiya'	מאפיה
written by	meet'	מאת
two hundred	mata'im	מאתים
preface, introduction	mavo'	מבוא
adult	mevugar'	מבוגר
insulator	mevoded'	מבודד
insulated	mevudad'	מבודד
wanted, popular (m.)	mevukash'	מבוקש
wanted, popular (f.)	mevuke'shet	מבוקשת
cooked	mevushal'	מבושל
test (n.)	mivkhan'	מבחן
look (n.)	mabat'	מבט
accent (n.)	mivta'	מבטא
controller	mevaker'	מבקר
screwdriver	mavreg'	מברג
brush (n.)	mivre'shet	מברשת
toothbrush	mivre'shet shina'im	מברשת שיניים
windshield wiper	magav'	מגב
towel	mage'vet	מגבת
slide (n.)	maglesha'	מגלשה
star of David	magen' david'	מגן דוד
emergency medical unit named Magen David	magen' david' adom'	מגן דוד אדום
magnet	magnet'	מגנט
touch (n.)	maga'	מגע
disgusting	mag"il'	מגעיל
boots	magafa'im	מגפיים
field	migrash'	מגרש
tray	magash'	מגש
thermometer	mad' khom	מד חום
desert (n.)	midbar'	מדבר
precise	meduyak'	מדויק
too	miday'	מדי
measurement	mdida'	מדידה
state (n.)	mdina'	מדינה
science	mada'	מדע
scientist	mad"an'	מדען
printer	madpe'set	מדפסת
stairs	madregot'	מדרגות
guide (m.)	madrikh'	מדריך
guide (f.)	madrikha'	מדריכה
what?	ma?	מה?
how are things?	ma nishma'?	מה נשמע?
how are you?	ma shlomkha'?	מה שלומך?

rapid (m.)	mahir’	מהיר
rapid (f.)	mhira’	מהירה
speed (n.)	mhirut’	מהירות
engineer	mehandes’	מהנדס
chief engineer	mehandes’ rashi’	מהנדס ראשי
fast, quickly	maher’	מהר
brought (m.)	muva’	מובא
clear, evident	muvan’ meelav’	מובן מאליו
limited	mugbal’	מוגבל
advertisement	modaa’	מודעה
information (office)	modiin’	מודעין
modern	moder’ni	מודרני
death	ma’vet	מוות
museum	museon’	מוזיאון
Israel Museum	muzeon’ israel’	מוזיאון ישראל
Rockefeller Museum	muzeon’ rokfe’ler	מוזיאון רוקפלר
invited	muzman’	מוזמן
strange	muzar’	מוזר
absolute	mukhlat’	מוחלט
pole	mot	מוט
ready (m.)	mukhan’	מוכן
ready (f.)	mukhana’	מוכנה
known, approved	mukar’	מוכר
salesman	mokher’	מוכר
saleswoman	mokhe’ret	מוכרת
dictated (m.)	mukhtav’	מוכתב
opposite	mul	מול
conductor	molikh’	מוליך
semi-conductor	molikh’ lemakhatsa’	מוליך למחצה
conductivity	molikhut’	מוליכות
taxi	monit’	מונית
music	mus’ika	מוסיקה
garage	mosakh’	מוסך
is (was) agreed	muskam’	מוסכם
club	moadon’	מועדון
night club	moadon’ layla’	מועדון לילה
useful	moil’	מועיל
surprised	mufta’	מופתע
exit; origin	motsa’	מוצא
focus (n.)	moked’	מוקד
early	mukdam’	מוקדם
teacher	more’	מורה
expanded	murkav’	מורכב
comprised of	murkav’ mi...	מורכב מ...
rural settlement	moshav’	מושב
attractive	moshekh’	מושך
governor	moshel’	מושל
sweet heart!	mo’tek!	מותק!
allowed	mutar’	מותר
may I?	mutar’ li?	מותר לי?

weather	me'zeg avir'	מזג אויר
air conditioner	mazgan'	מזגן
suitcase (suitcases)	mizvada' (mizvadot')	מזוודה (מזוודות)
cash (n.)	mezuman'	מזומן
souvenirs	mazkerot'	מזכרות
luck	mazal'	מזל
fork	mazleg'	מזלג
mattress	mizron'	מזרון
east	mizrakh'	מזרח
notebook	makhbe'ret	מחברת
rough	mekhuspas'	מחוספס
calculated	mekhushav'	מחושב
cycle, period	makhzor'	מחזור
periodical	makhzori'	מחזורי
needle	ma'khat	מחט
price	mkhir'	מחיר
dairy	makhleva'	מחלבה
disease	makhala'	מחלה
heart diseases	makhalot' lev	מחלות לב
infectious diseases	makhalot' medabkot'	מחלות מדבקות
skin disorders	makhalot' or	מחלות עור
dispute (n.)	makhlo'ket	מחלוקת
compliment (n.)	makhmaa'	מחמאה
camp (n.)	makhane'	מחנה
stuffy, suffocating	makhnik'	מחניק
barrier	makhsom'	מחסום
storeroom	makhsan'	מחסן
tomorrow	makhar'	מחר
day after tomorrow	mokhrota'im	מחרתיים
computer, PC	makhshev' ishi'	מחשב אישי
thought	makhshava'	מחשבה
calculator	makhshevon'	מחשבון
kitchen	mitbakh'	מטבח
coin	matbe'a	מטבע
plane, airplane	matos'	מטוס
plantation	mata'	מטע
load (n.)	mit"an'	מטען
lift, cargo	mit"an'	מטען
luggage	mit"an'	מטען
aim, target (n.)	matara'	מטרה
umbrella	metriya'	מטריה
who?	mi?	מי?
whoever	mi she...	מי ש...
drinking water	mey shtiya'	מי שתיה
immediately	miyad'	מיד
immediate	miyadi'	מידי
information	meyda'	מידע
despondent (m.)	meyuash'	מיואש
despondent (f.)	meyue'shet	מיואשת
classification	miyun'	מיון

settled, inhabited	meyushav'	מיושב
unnecessary	meyutar'	מיותר
bed	mita'	מיטה
tank, container	meykhal'	מיכל
word	mila'	מילה
dictionary	milon'	מילון
million	mil"yon'	מיליון
water	ma'im	מים
hot water	ma'im khamim'	מים חמים
tepid water	ma'im poshrim'	מים פושרים
cold water	ma'im karim'	מים קרים
sex, kind (n.)	min	מין
sexual	mi'ni	מיני
minimum	mi'nimum	מינימום
minority	miut'	מיעוט
juice	mits	מיץ
microscope	mikroskop'	מיקרוסקופ
microphone	mikrofon'	מיקרופון
wish (n.)	mish"ala'	מישאלה
someone	mi'shehu	מישהו
corner shop, grocery	mako'let	מכולת
mechanic	mekhonai'	מכונאי
machine	mekhona'	מכונה
car	mekhonit'	מכונית
washing machine	mekhonat' kvisa'	מכונת כביסה
addicted to	makhur' le...	מכור ל...
sale (n.)	mkhira'	מכירה
trousers, pants	mikhnasa'im	מכנסיים
customs	me'khes	מכס
instrument	makhshir'	מכשיר
electrical appliances	makhshirey' khashmal'	מכשירי חשמל
letter	mikhtav'	מכתב
full	male'	מלא
angel	mal"akh'	מלאך
salty	malu'akh, mlukha'	מלוח, מלוחה
dirty (m.)	melukhlakh'	מלוכלך
dirty (f.)	melukhle'khet	מלוכלכת
scholarly	melumad'	מלומד
hotel	malon'	מלון
melon	melon'	מלון
salt	me'lakh	מלח
sailor	malakh'	מלח
war	milkhama'	מלחמה
cucumber	melafefon'	מלפפון
waiter	meltsar'	מלצר
waitress	meltsarit'	מלצרית
average	memutsa'	ממוצע
bastard	mamzer'	ממזר
government	memshala'	ממשלה
since when?	meymatay'?	ממתי?

from	min, me...	מן, מ...
from then	meaz'	מאז
from where	meey'fo	מאיפה
from where do (did) you	meey'fo ata'...	מאיפה אתה...
from school	mebeyt' hase'fer	מבית הספר
from the morning...	mehabo'ker...	מהבוקר...
from the house	mehaba'yt	מהבית
from the building	mehabin"yan'	מהבנין
from the chair	mehakise'	מהכיסא
from the stairs	mehamadregot'	מהמדרגות
from the evening...	mehae'rev...	מהערב...
from the table	mehashulkhan'	מהשולחן
from here	mikan'	מכאן
from all this	mikol' ze	מכל זה
from everything	mikol' hainyanim'	מכל הענינים
from below	milma'ta	מלמטה
from above	milma'la	מלמעלה
from what	mima'	ממה
from work	meavoda'	מעבודה
from there	misham'	משם
from under	mita'khat le...	מתחת ל...
apparatus	manganon'	מנגנון
portion	mana'	מנה
main course	mana' ikarit'	מנה עיקרית
appetizer	mana' rishona'	מנה ראשונה
second portion	mana' shniya'	מנה שניה
leader	manhig'	מנהיג
manager, principal	menahel'	מנהל
production manager	menahel' yetsur'	מנהל ייצור
rest (n.)	menukha'	מנוחה
motor, engine	manu'a	מנוע
lamp	menora'	מנורה
reasonable, acceptable	mani'yakh et hada'at	מניח את הדעת
lock (n.)	man"ul'	מנעול
tax (n.)	mas	מס
all around	mesaviv'	מסביב
around the corner	mesaviv' lapina'	מסביב לפינה
mosque	misgad'	מסגד
metalworker	masger'	מסגר
frame (n.)	misge'ret	מסגרת
able	mesugal'	מסוגל
orderly, neat	mesudar'	מסודר
certain	mesuyam'	מסוים
dangerous	mesukan'	מסוכן
trade (n.)	miskhar'	מסחר
commercial	miskhari'	מסחרי
mask (n.)	masekha'	מסכה
path	maslul'	מסלול

documents	mismakhim'	מסמכים
nail (nails)	masmer' (masmerim')	מסמר (מסמרים)
restaurant	mis"ada'	מסעדה
enough	maspik'	מספיק
number (n.)	mispar'	מספר
salon, barbershop	mispara'	מספרה
comb (n.)	masrek'	מסרק
processor, microprocessor	meabed'	מעבד
food processor	meabed' mazon'	מעבד מזון
laboratory	maabada'	מעבדה
across	mee'ver	מעבר
passage, transition	maavar'	מעבר
processed	meubad'	מעובד
few, a few, a little	meat'	מעט
too little	meat' miday'	מעט מדי
envelope	maatafa'	מעטפה
coat	meil'	מעיל
above	meal', meal' le...	מעל, מעל ל...
degree	maala'	מעלה
status	maamad'	מעמד
answer (n.), response	maane'	מענה
interesting	meanyen'	מענין
grant (n.)	maanak'	מענק
follow-up	maakav'	מעקב
west	maarav'	מערב
act (n.)	maase'	מעשה
practical	maasi '	מעשי
map, tablecloth	mapa'	מפה
map of the city	mapa' shel ha'ir	מפה של העיר
scary	mafkhid'	מפחיד
level	miflas'	מפלס
because of what?	mipney' ma?	מפני מה?
circuit breaker	mafsek'	מפסק
plant, factory	mif"al'	מפעל
key	mafte'yakh	מפתח
situation	matsav'	מצב
mood, bad mood	matsav' ru'akh	מצב רוח
voters	matsbiim'	מצביעים
excellent, perfect, excellently, very well, fine	metsuyan'	מצוין
forehead	me'tsakh	מצח
sorry!	mitstaer'!	מצטער!
bargain (n.)	mtsia'	מציאה
successful	matsli'yakh	מצליח
camera	matslema'	מצלמה
conscience	matspun'	מצפון
compass	matspen'	מצפן
Egypt	mitsra'im	מצרים

sale item	mitsrakh'	מצרך
provisions	mitsrakhim'	מצרכים
drill bit	makde'yakh	מקדח
drill (n.)	makdekha'	מקדחה
coefficient, factor	mekadem'	מקדם
usual	mekubal'	מקובל
accepted	mekubal'	מקובל
accepted (m.)	mekubal'	מקובל
accepted (f.)	mekube'let	מקובלת
spoiled (m.)	mekulkal'	מקולקל
spoiled (f.)	mekulke'let	מקולקלת
place (n.), room	makom'	מקום
source	makor'	מקור
authority	makor' musmakh'	מקור מוסמך
stick (n.)	makel'	מקל
keyboard	makle'det	מקלדת
shower (n.)	mikla'khat	מקלחת
profession	miktso'a	מקצוע
professional	miktsoi'	מקצועי
refrigerator	mekarer'	מקרר
sight	mar''e'	מראה
mirror	mar''a'	מראה
exciting	meragesh	מרגש
space (n.)	mirvakh'	מרווח
interval	mirvakh' zman	מרווח זמן
satisfied	merutse'	מרוצה
from a distance	merakhok'	מרחוק
distance	merkhak'	מרחק
center	merkaz'	מרכז
elbow	marpek'	מרפק
March	merts	מרץ
lecturer	martse'	מרצה
soup	marak'	מרק
truck	masait'	משאית
satisfactory	masbi'a ratson'	משביע רצון
something	ma'shehu	משהו
something else	ma'shehu akher'	משהו אחר
something strange	ma'shehu muzar'	משהו מוזר
something suitable	ma'shehu mat''im'	משהו מתאים
saw (n.)	masor'	משור
poet	meshorer'	משורר
joint	meshutaf'	משותף
grinder	mashkhe'zet	משחזת
game, play (n.)	miskhak'	משחק
police	mishtara'	משטרה
police department	mishtara'	משטרה
traffic police	mishte'ret tnua'	משטרת תנועה
silk	me'shi	משי
attraction	mshikha'	משיכה
duration	me'shekh	משך

lying down	mishkav'	משכב
salary	masko'ret	משכורת
parable, allegory (n.)	mashal'	משל
boring	meshaamem'	משעמם
family	mishpakha'	משפחה
farm (n.)	me'shek	משק
weight	mishkal'	משקל
office, ministry	misrad'	משרד
Ministry of the Interior	misrad' hapnim'	משרד הפנים
Ministry of Tourism	misrad' hatayarut'	משרד התיירות
dead, corpse	met	מת
sweet (m.)	matok'	מתוק
sweet (f.)	metuka'	מתוקה
tension	me'takh	מתח
considering that	mitkhashev' be...	מתחשב ב...
under	mita'khat	מתחת
when	matay'	מתי
mean	mitkaven'	מתכוון
metal	mate'khet	מתכת
metallic	matakhti'	מתכתי
mathematics	matema'tika	מתמטיקה
mathematician	matematika'i	מתמטיקאי
opposition	mitnagdim'	מתנגדים
present (n.)	matana'	מתנה
snob	mitnase'	מתנשא
fainting	mit"alef'	מתעלף
rowdy (m.)	mitpare'a	מתפרע
rowdy (f.)	mitpara'at	מתפרעת
progressive	mitkadem'	מתקדם

נ

please	na	נא
come in!	na lehikanes'!	נא להכנס!
please listen	na lehakshiv'	נא להקשיב
please sit down	na lashe'vet	נא לשבת
let's say that	nomar' she...	נאמר ש...
prophet	navi'	נביא
anti	ne'ged	נגד
against	ne'ged	נגד
counterclockwise	ne'ged kivun' hashaon'	נגד כיוון השעון
resistor	nagad'	נגד
carpenter	nagar'	נגר
generous (m.)	nadiv'	נדיב
generous (f.)	nediva'	נדיבה
rare (m.)	nadir'	נדיר
apparently	nidme'	נדמה
got screwed	nidfak'	נדפק
in demand	nidrash'	נדרש
driver	nahag'	נהג

wonderful, great	nehedar′	נהדר
river	nahar′	נהר
November	nove′mber	נובמבר
nudnik, pest	nud′nik	נודניק
oasis	nave′ midbar′	נווה מדבר
liquid	nozel′	נוזל
version	nu′sakh	נוסח
passenger	nose′a	נוסע
awful!	nora′!	נורא!
light bulb	nura′	נורה
normal	norma′li	נורמלי
copper	nekho′shet	נחושת
determination	nekhishut′	נחישות
flight arrival	nekhita′	נחיתה
snake (snakes)	nakhash′ (nakhashim′)	נחש (נחשים)
burden (n.)	ne′tel	נטל
conflict (n.)	nigud′	ניגוד
neutral	neitra′li	נייטרלי
paper	n"yar′	נייר
tape (n.)	n"yar′ de′vek	נייר דבק
toilet paper	n"yar′ tualet′	נייר טואלט
reason, excuse	nimuk′	נימוק
survivor	nitsol′	ניצול
exploitation	nitsul′	ניצול
victory	nitsakhon′	ניצחון
grandson	ne′khed	נכד
granddaughter	nekhda′	נכדה
right, correct, correctly, true	nakhon′	נכון
entered	nikhnas′	נכנס
low, short	namukh′	נמוך
is sold	nimkar′	נמכר
port	namal′	נמל
airport	namal′ teufa′	נמל תעופה
ant (ants)	nemala′ (nemalim′)	נמלה (נמלים)
melting	names′	נמס
is found (m.)	nimtsa′	נמצא
is found (f.)	nimtsea′	נמצאה
let's suppose	nani′akh	נניח
instant coffee	nes kafe′	נס קפה
withdrawal	nesiga′	נסיגה
journey	nesia′	נסיעה
upset (adj.)	nis"ar′	נסער
slippers	naaley′ ba′yt	נעלי בית
shoes	naala′im	נעליים
adolescent	na′ar	נער
wounded	nifga′	נפגע
fall, collapse	nefila′	נפילה
marvelous	nifla′	נפלא
representative	natsig′	נציג

female	nekeva'	נקבה
point (n.)	nekuda'	נקודה
that's final!	nekuda'!	נקודה !
electrical outlet	nekudat' khashmal'	נקודת חשמל
clean (m.)	naki '	נקי
clean (f.)	nekiya'	נקיה
very clean	naki ' naki '	נקי נקי
knock (n.)	nekisha'	נקישה
revenge	nekama'	נקמה
salami	naknik'	נקניק
frankfurter	naknikiya'	נקניקיה
candle	ner	נר
seems	nir''e'	נראה
asleep	nirdam'	נרדם
married (m.)	nasu'y	נשוי
married (f.)	nesua'	נשואה
President	nasi'	נשיא
it sounds good	nishma' tov	נשמע טוב
disconnection	ne'tek	נתק
encountered difficulties	nitkal' bekshaim'	נתקל בקשיים

ס

grandfather	sa'ba	סבה
soap	sabon'	סבון
around	saviv', saviv' le...	סביב, סביב ל...
environment	sviva'	סביבה
passive	savil'	סביל
reasonable	savir'	סביר
porter	sabal'	סבל
grandmother	sav'ta	סבתא
closed	sagur'	סגור
closing	sgira'	סגירה
sheet (sheets)	sadin' (sdinim')	סדין (סדינים)
order (n.)	se'der	סדר
certain type	sug mesuyam'	סוג מסוים
parentheses	sogra'im	סוגריים
secret	sod	סוד
sweater	sve'der	סוודר
agency	sokhnut'	סוכנות
travel agency	sokhnut ' nesiyot '	סוכנות נסיעות
travel agent (only f.)	sokhe'net nesiyot '	סוכנת נסיעות
sugar	sukar'	סוכר
ladder	sulam'	סולם
horse (horses)	sus' (susim')	סוס (סוסים)
work horse	sus avoda'	סוס עבודה
end (n.)	sof	סוף
finally	sof sof	סוף סוף
in the end	sofo' shel davar'	סופו של דבר

writer	sofer′	סופר
supermarket	supermar′ket	סופרמרקט
contradicts himself	soter′ et atsmo′	סותר את עצמו
goods	skhu′ra	סחורה
student (m.)	student′	סטודנט
student (f.)	studen′tit	סטודנטית
deviation, deflection	stiya′	סטייה
steak	stek′	סטיק
contradiction	stira′	סטירה
slap in the face	stirat′ le′khi	סטירת לחי
reason (n.)	siba′	סיבה
fiber	siv	סיב
pin (n.)	sika′	סיכה
sign, mark	siman′	סימן
conventional sign	siman′ mekubal′	סימן מקובל
question mark	siman′ sheela′	סימן שאלה
story	sipur′	סיפור
fictitious story	sipur′ badu′y	סיפור בדוי
pot	sir	סיר
total sum	sakh hakol′	סך הכל
amount	skhum	סכום
knife (knives)	sakin′ (sakinim′)	סכין (סכינים)
danger	sakana′	סכנה
basket	sal	סל
living room	salon′	סלון
sorry, forgive me	slakh′ li	סלח לי
salad	salat′	סלט
excuse me! pardon me!	slikha′!	סליחה!
beet	se′lek	סלק
alley	simta′	סמטה
rag	smartut′	סמרטוט
sandals	sanda′lim	סנדלים
paragraph	seif′	סעיף
storm	seara′	סערה
commotion	saarat′ rukhot′	סערת רוחות
sponge	sfog′	ספוג
September	septem′ber	ספטמבר
ship (n.)	sfina′	ספינה
counting	sfira′	ספירה
countdown	sfira′ leakhor′	ספירה לאחור
mug	se′fel	ספל
barber	sapar′	ספר
book (books)	se′fer (sfarim′)	ספר (ספרים)
school book	se′fer limud′	ספר לימוד
figure, digit(s)	sifra′ (sifrot′)	ספרה (ספרות)
literature	sifrut′	ספרות
library	sifriya′	ספריה
film, movie	se′ret	סרט
suspense movie	se′ret me′takh	סרט מתח

bruise (n.)	srita'	סריטה
autumn	stav	סתו
just (adv.)	stam	סתם

ע

thick (m.)	ave'	עבה
thick (f.)	ava'	עבה
job, work	avoda'	עבודה
sin, offence	avera'	עבירה
past	avar'	עבר
tomato	agvaniya'	עגבניה
round (m.)	agol'	עגול
round (f.)	agula'	עגולה
cart	agala'	עגלה
witness (n.) (m.)	ed	עד
witness (n.) (f.)	eda'	עדה
until, up to	ad	עד
until then	ad az'	עד אז
till the end, until the end	ad hasof'	עד הסוף
until here	ad kan'	עד כאן
until now	ad ko'	עד כה
until when?	ad matay'?	עד מתי?
update	idkun'	עדכון
worker	oved'	עובד
fact, it's a fact	uvda'	עובדה
thickness	o'vi	עובי
cake	uga'	עוגה
cookies	ugiyot'	עוגיות
distress (n.)	ugmat' ne'fesh	עוגמת נפש
anchor (n.)	o'gen	עוגן
more, still	od	עוד
not yet	od lo	עוד לא
we'll yet see	od nir"e'	עוד נראה
yet	od, ada'yin	עוד, עדיין
bit more, a bit more	od ktsat'	עוד קצת
change (money)	o'def	עודף
helper	ozer'	עוזר
maid	oze'ret	עוזרת
hostile	oyen'	עוין
antagonism	oyenut'	עוינות
world	olam'	עולם
universal	olami'	עולמי
depth	o'mek	עומק
season	una'	עונה
the bathing season	onat' harakhatsa'	עונת הרחצה
chicken	of	עוף
intensity, force	otsma'	עוצמה
curfew	o'tser	עוצר

skin, leather	or	עור
editor	orekh'	עורך
lawyer	o'rekh din	עורך דין
copy (n.)	o'tek	עותק
forget it! leave it alone!	azov' et ze!	עזוב את זה!
goats	izim'	עזים
helping	e'zer	עזר
help (n.)	ezra'	עזרה
financial assistance	ezra' kaspit'	עזרה כספית
pen	et	עט
processing	ibud'	עיבוד
circle	igul'	עיגול
tired (m.)	ayef'	עייף
tired (f.)	ayefa'	עייפה
delay (n.)	ikuv'	עיכוב
conflict (n.)	imut'	עימות
eye (eyes)	a'yin (eyna'im)	עין (עיניים)
occupation	isuk'	עיסוק
pencil	iparon'	עיפרון
primary	ikari'	עיקרי
city, town	ir	עיר
capital city	ir habira'	עיר הבירה
Old City of Jerusalem	ir haatika'	עיר העתיקה
newspaper	iton'	עיתון
mouse, mice	akhbar (akhbarim')	עכבר (עכברים)
now	akhshav'	עכשיו
about, on	al	על
even more so	al akhat' ka'ma vekha'ma	על אחת כמה וכמה
on the ground	al haadama'	על האדמה
by	al yedey'	על ידי
about it	al kakh'	על כך
about what?	al ma?	על מה?
on the basis of	al smakh'	על סמך
on what basis?	al smakh ma'?	על סמך מה?
on the beach	al sfat hayam'	על שפת הים
on condition, on probation	al tnay'	על תנאי
leaf	ale'	עלה
rose (v.)	ala'	עלה
(he) was able	ala' beyadav'	עלה בידיו
cost him a lot	ala' lo beyo'ker	עלה לו ביוקר
cost (n.)	alut'	עלות
increase (n.)	aliya'	עליה
about her	aley'ha	עליה
about him	alav'	עליו
upper	el"yon'	עליון
nation	am	עם
with	im	עם

hesitatingly	im hisusim'	עם היסוסים
stand (v.)	amad'	עמד
kept his promise	amad' behavtakhato'	עמד בהבטחתו
passed the test	amad' bamivkhan'	עמד במבחן
attitude, position, stand (n.)	emda'	עמדה
page	amud'	עמוד
attention!	amod' dom!	עמוד דום!
column	amuda'	עמודה
deep	amok'	עמוק
wealthy	amida'	עמידה
masses	am'kha	עמך
labor (n.)	amal'	עמל
grape(s)	anavim'	ענבים
poor (m.)	ani'	עני
poor (f.)	aniya'	עניה
matter, interest	inyan'	ענין
cloud (clouds)	anan' (ananim')	ענן (עננים)
busy	asuk'	עסוק
deal (n.)	iska'	עסקה
business	asakim'	עסקים
tree(s), wood(s)	ets (etsim')	עץ (עצים)
olive trees	atsey' za'it	עצי זית
fruit trees	atsey' pri	עצי פרי
nerve; sadness	e'tsev	עצב
nerves, patience	atsabim'	עצבים
advice	etsa'	עצה
sad	atsuv'	עצוב
tremendous, great	atsum'	עצום
stop!	atsor'!	עצור!
bone(s)	e'tsem, atsamot'	עצם, עצמות
independence	atsmaut'	עצמאות
independent	atsmai'	עצמאי
heel	e'kev	עקב
scorpion (scorpions)	akrab' (akrabim')	עקרב (עקרבים)
stubborn (m.)	akshan'	עקשן
stubborn (f.)	akshanit'	עקשנית
awake (m.)	er	ער
awake (f.)	era'	ערה
evening	e'rev	ערב
Arab	aravi'	ערבי
value (values)	e'rekh (arakhim')	ערך (ערכים)
moth	ash	עש
done	asu'i	עשוי
may rise	asui' laalot'	עשוי לעלות
doing, acting, activity	asiya'	עשיה
rich (m.)	ashir'	עשיר
rich (f.)	ashira'	עשירה
tenth	asiri'	עשירי
smoke (n.)	ashan'	עשן

ten (f.)	e'ser	עשר
ten (m.)	asara'	עשרה
ten thousand	ase'ret alafim'	עשרת אלפים
twenty	esrim'	עשרים
time (n.)	et	עת
reserve (n.)	atuda'	עתודה
future	atid'	עתיד

פ

pub	pub	פאב
February	fe'bruar	פברואר
premature infant	pag	פג
expired	pag to'kef	פג תוקף
damaged	pagum'	פגום
hit (n.)	pgia'	פגיעה
meeting, appointment	pgisha'	פגישה
defect	pgam'	פגם
turnover, redemption	pid"yon'	פדיון
mouth	pe	פה
unanimous	pe ekhad'	פה אחד
here	po	פה
right here	po bamakom'	פה במקום
here and there	po vesham'	פה ושם
bean	pul	פול
inn	pundak'	פונדק
worker	poel'	פועל
construction worker	poel' binyan'	פועל בנין
the result of	po'al yotse' min	פועל יוצא מן
opener	potkhan'	פותחן
tin	pakh	פח
sheet metal	pakh	פח
less	pakhot'	פחות
can	pakhit'	פחית
hammer	patish'	פטיש
raspberry, raspberry drink	pe'tel	פטל
division, dissention	pilug'	פילוג
physics	fi 'sika	פיסיקה
sculpture	pisul'	פיסול
physicist	fizika'i	פיסיקאי
deposit (n.)	pikadon'	פיקדון
development	pitu'akh	פיתוח
wonder (n.)	pe'le	פלא
cell phone	pe'lefon	פלאפון
steel	plada'	פלדה
emission	plita'	פליטה
pliers	pla'yer	פלייר
pepper	pilpel'	פלפל
felafel	fala'fel	פלפל

side (n.)	pan	פן
surface	pney she'takh	פני שטח
interior	pnim	פנים
face (n.)	panim'	פנים
inside	pni'ma	פנימה
internal	pnimi'	פנימי
inner tube	pnimit'	פנימית
full board	pension' male'	פנסיון מלא
flat tire	pan'cher	פנצ'ר
notebook, ledger	pinkas'	פנקס
checkbook	pinkas' tche'kim	פנקס שקים
stripe	pas	פס
piano	psanter'	פסנתר
verdict, judgment	psak din'	פסק דין
pause (n.)	pe'sek zman	פסק זמן
nursery	peuton'	פעוטון
once	pa'am	פעם
time after time	pa'am akharey' pa'am	פעם אחרי פעם
another time	paam' akhe'ret	פעם אחרת
twice	paama'im	פעמיים
several times	peamim' akhadot',	פעמים אחדות,
	ka'ma peamim'	כמה פעמים
gap	pa'ar	פער
growing gap	pa'ar holekh' vegodel'	פער הולך וגודל
wounded	patsu'a	פצוע
wound (n.)	pe'tsa	פצע
clerk (m.)	pakid'	פקיד
clerk (f.)	pkida'	פקידה
animal! wild thing!	pe're adam'!	פרא אדם!
cow (cows)	para (parot)	פרה (פרות)
slice (n.)	prusa'	פרוסה
wild	paru'a	פרוע
fruit (fruits)	pri (perot')	פרי (פרות)
flower (flowers)	pe'rakh (prakhim')	פרח (פרחים)
detail	prat	פרט
except for	prat le...	פרט ל...
other than this	prat le ze	פרט לזה
except for that	prat lekhakh'	פרט לכך
private	prati'	פרטי
plain, simple	pashut'	פשוט
blooper	fash'la	פשלה
suddenly	pit"om'	פתאום
open (adj.)(adv.)	patu'akh	פתוח
entrance	pe'takh	פתח
opening	pati'yakh	פתיח
opening	ptikha'	פתיחה
solution	pitaron'	פתרון

צ

get out	tse	צא
get out of here!	tse mikan'!	צא מכאן!
army	tsava'	צבא
military	tsvai'	צבאי
hypocrite	tsavu'a	צבוע
painting	tsvia'	צביעה
color	tse'va	צבע
sabra	tsabar'	צבר
side, part	tsad	צד
side by side	tsad betsad'	צד בצד
right side	tsad yamin'	צד ימין
certain aspect	tsad mesuyam'	צד מסוים
left side	tsad smol	צד שמאל
righteous	tsa'dik	צדיק
justice	tse'dek	צדק
charity	tsdaka'	צדקה
yellow	tsahov', tsehuba'	צהוב, צהובה
noon, afternoon, midday	tsohoray'im	צהרים
order (n.)	tsav	צו
enlistment orders	tsav giyus'	צו גיוס
excrement	tsoa'	צואה
neck	tsavar'	צואר
will, testament	tsvaa'	צוואה
inch	tsol	צול
submarine	tsole'let	צוללת
shape (n.)	tsura'	צורה
need (n.)	tso'rekh	צורך
laugh (n.)	tskhok	צחוק
equipment	tsiyud'	ציוד
art	tsiyur'	ציור
artist	tsayar'	צייר
photograph, photography	tsilum'	צילום
x-ray	tsilum' rent'gen	צילום רנטגן
bed and breakfast	tsi'mer	צימר
prison, confinement	tsinok'	צינוק
pipe	tsinor'	צינור
pillowcase(s)	tsipa' (tsipot')	ציפה (ציפות)
bird	tsipor'	ציפור
fingernails	tsiporna'im	ציפורניים
French fries	tchips	ציפס
axis	tsir	ציר
shadow (shadows)	tsel (tslalim')	צל (צללים)
slight hesitation	tsel shel hisus'	צל של היסוס
award (n.)	tsalash'	צל״ש
plate	tsala'khat	צלחת
roast (n.)	tsli'	צלי

diving	tslila'	צלילה
photographer	tsalam'	צלם
humanity	tse'lem enosh'	צלם אנוש
plant (n.)	tse'makh	צמח
tire (n.)	tsamig'	צמיג
bracelet	tsamid'	צמיד
growth	tsmikha'	צמיחה
wool	tse'mer	צמר
shivers (n.)	tsmarmo'ret	צמרמורת
tree-top; upper class	tsame'ret	צמרת
modest (m.)	tsanu'a	צנוע
modest (f.)	tsnua'	צנועה
young (m.)	tsair'	צעיר
young (f.)	tseira'	צעירה
toy	tsaatsu'a	צעצוע
north	tsafon'	צפון
crowded	tsafuf'	צפוף
expectation	tsfiya'	צפיה
density	tsfifut'	צפיפות
siren	tsfira'	צפירה
check (n.)	chek	צ׳ק
narrow	tsar	צר
need (have)	tsarikh'	צריך
needs (has) to be	tsarikh' lih"yot'	צריך להיות
needs (has) to do	tsarikh' laasot'	צריך לעשות
consumption	tsrikha'	צריכה

ק

permanent	kavu'a	קבוע
group	kvutsa'	קבוצה
burial	kvura'	קבורה
permanence, tenure	kviut'	קביעות
openly, publicly	kval am veeda'	קבל עם ועדה
reception, receipt	kabala'	קבלה
decision-making	kabalat' hakhlata'	קבלת החלטה
reception	kabalat' panim'	קבלת פנים
welcoming the Sabbath	kabalat' shabat'	קבלת שבת
grave	ke'ver	קבר
forward	kadi'ma	קדימה
community	kehilla'	קהילה
audience	kahal'	קהל
former, previous	kodem'	קודם
first of all	ko'dem kol	קודם כל
diameter	ko'ter	קוטר
voice	kol	קול
loud	kolani'	קולני
get up!	kum!	קום!
get up already!	kum kvar!	קום כבר!

kettle	kumkum'	קומקום
buyer	kone'	קונה
cognac	ko'n"yak	קוניק
concert	kontsert'	קונצרט
cashier	kupai '	קופאי
cash register	kupa'	קופה
box	kufsa'	קופסה
clinic, sick fund	kupat ' kholim'	קופת חולים
curriculum vitae	korot' khayim'	קורות חיים
difficulty	ko'shi	קושי
casino	kazi'no	קזינו
harvest (n.)	katif'	קטיף
small	katan'	קטן
ketchup	ket'chup	קטצ'ופ
capacity	kibo'let	קיבולת
existence	kiyum'	קיום
kilo	ki 'lo	קילו
summer	ka'yts	קיץ
wall	kir	קיר
squash (n.)	kishuim'	קישואים
easy	kal	קל
light (m.)	kal	קל
light (f.)	kala'	קלה
clutch (n.)	klyach'	קלאץ'
calories	kalo'riot	קלוריות
absorption	klita'	קליטה
curse (n.)	klala'	קללה
tangerine oranges	klemanti'not	קלמנטינות
card	klaf	קלף
playing cards	klafim'	קלפים
stingy	kamtsan'	קמצן
purchase (n.)	kniya'	קניה
mall	kanyion'	קניון
cinnamon	kinamon'	קנמון
fine (penalty)	knas	קנס
bowl	keara'	קערה
cafe, coffee	kafe'	קפה
spring (n.)	kfits	קפיץ
jump (n.)	kfitsa'	קפיצה
rhythm	ke'tsev	קצב
edge	katse'	קצה
officer (m.)	katsin'	קצין
patties	ktsitsot '	קציצות
fuse	ke'tser	קצר
breakdown in	ke'tser be...	קצר ב...
short	katsar'	קצר
a bit	ktsat'	קצת
cold	kar	קר
battle	krav	קרב
vicinity, closeness	kirva'	קרבה

near	karov'	קרוב
most probably	karov' levaday'	קרוב לוודאי
relatives	krovey' mishpakha'	קרובי משפחה
ice	ke'rakh	קרח
cardboard	karton'	קרטון
reading	kria'	קריאה
critical	kri'ti	קריטי
announcer	kar"yan'	קריין
broadcaster	kar"yan'	קריין
radiation	krina'	קרינה
collapse (n.)	krisa'	קריסה
tearing, rending	kria'	קריעה
cool	karir'	קריר
body lotion	krem guf	קרם גוף
suntan lotion	krem shizuf'	קרם שיזוף
ray	ke'ren	קרן
ankle	karsul'	קרסול
circus	kirkas'	קרקס
land (n.)	kar'ka	קרקע
bottom	karkait'	קרקעית
plank	ke'resh	קרש
hard, difficult	kashe'	קשה
particularly difficult	kashe' bim"yukhad'	קשה במיוחד
hard to know	kashe' lada'at	קשה לדעת
hard to understand	kashe lehavin'	קשה להבין
connection	ke'sher	קשר
very close connection	ke'sher haduk'	קשר הדוק
bow, rainbow, arc	ke'shet	קשת

ר

suitable	rau'y	ראוי
visibility	re"ut'	ראות
mirror	rei'	ראי
vision	reiya'	ראיה
foresight	reiya' mefuka'khat	ראיה מפוקחת
interview	raayon'	ראיון
mind, head	rosh	ראש
prime minister	rosh hamemshala'	ראש הממשלה
first	rishon'	ראשון
chief, major (adj.)	rashi'	ראשי
first of all	reshit'	ראשית
rabbi	rav	רב
fourth	rvii'	רביעי
quarter	re'va	רבע
ordinary, regular	ragil'	רגיל
used to	ragil' le...	רגיל ל...
sensitive	ragish'	רגיש
leg, foot	re'gel	רגל
feet	ragla'im	רגליים

don't bother me!	red mime'ni!	רד ממני!
shallow	radud'	רדוד
radiator	radia'tor	רדיאטור
radio	ra'dio	רדיו
furniture	rehitim'	רהיטים
accountant	roe' kheshbon'	רואה חשבון
is pessimistic	roe' shkhorot'	רואה שחורות
majority, most	rov	רוב
most people	rov haanashim'	רוב האנשים
most of the time	rov hazman'	רוב הזמן
great majority	rov makhri'a	רוב מכריע
profit	re'vakh	רווח
welfare	rvakha'	רווחה
saturation	revaya'	רוויה
windy	ru'akh	רוח
width	ro'khav	רוחב
spiritual	rukhani'	רוחני
sauce	ro'tev	רוטב
rotation	rota'tsiya	רוטציה
doctor (m.)	rofe'	רופא
dentist	rofe' shina'im	רופא שיניים
doctor (f.)	rof"a'	רופאה
loose	rofef'	רופף
impression	ro'shem	רושם
boiling	rote'aykh	רותח
broad, wide	rakhav'	רחב
street	rkhov'	רחוב
far	rakhok'	רחוק
wet	ratuv'	רטוב
dampness	retivut'	רטיבות
fruit jam	riba'	ריבה
square	ribu'a	ריבוע
concentration	rikuz'	ריכוז
sprint, run	ritsa'	ריצה
empty (adj.)	reyk	ריק
rot (n.)	rikavon'	ריקבון
dance (dances)	rikud' (rikudim')	ריקוד (ריקודים)
weld (n.)	ritukh'	ריתוך
soft	rakh	רך
vehicle	re'khev	רכב
railway, train	rake'vet	רכבת
bad	ra	רע
very bad	ra meod'	רע מאוד
hungry	raev'	רעב
hunger (n.)	ra'av	רעב
friendship	reut'	רעות
wife	reaya'	רעיה
idea	raayon'	רעיון
vibration	reidot'	רעידות
earthquake	reidat' adama'	רעידת אדמה

poison	ra'al	רעל
thunder	ra'am	רעם
fresh	raanan'	רענן
noise	ra'ash	רעש
medicine	refua'	רפואה
stable	re'fet	רפת
desirable	ratsu'y	רצוי
you should know	ratsu'y sheteda'	רצוי שתדע
murder (n.)	re'tsakh	רצח
only, just	rak	רק
sky	raki'a	רקיע
driver's license	rish"yon' nehiga'	רשיון נהיגה
careless	rashlan'	רשלן
grid	re'shet	רשת
welder	ratakh'	רתך
welding machine	rate'khet	רתכת

ש

question (n.)	sheela'	שאלה
your question	sheelatkha'	שאלתך
questionnaire	sheelon'	שאלון
sit down! sit!	shev!	שב!
sit quietly	shev beshe'ket	שב בשקט!
week	shavu'a	שבוע
weekly magazine	shvuon'	שבועון
two weeks	shvua'im	שבועיים
broken	shavur'	שבור
seventh	shvii'	שביעי
strike (n.)	shvita'	שביתה
seventeen	shva esre'	שבע עשרה
seven	shiv"a'	שבעה
seventy	shiv"im'	שבעים
seven thousand	shiv"at' alafim'	שבעת אלפים
fracture	she'ver	שבר
Sabbath, Saturday	shabat'	שבת
ambassador	shagrir'	שגריר
demon, devil	shed	שד
field	sade'	שדה
breasts	shida'im	שדיים
message, broadcaster	she'der	שדר
again	shuv	שוב
naughty (m.)	shovav'	שובב
naughty (f.)	shoveva'	שובבה
voucher	shovar'	שובר
striker	shovet'	שובת
robbery	shod	שוד
bandit	shoded'	שודד
worthwhile	shave'	שווה
equality	shiv"yon'	שוויון

roasted meat in pita	shvar'ma	שוורמה
policeman	shoter'	שוטר
table (tables)	shulkhan' (shulkhanot')	שולחן (שולחנות)
marginal	shuli'	שולי
completely incidental	shuli' legam're	שולי לגמרי
garlic	shum	שום
nothing new	shum davar' khadash'	שום דבר חדש
fat *(n.)*	shoman'	שומן
do you hear?	shome'a?	שומע?
watchman	shomer'	שומר
different	shone'	שונה
difference	sho'ni	שוני
judge (n.)	shofet'	שופט
market (n.)	shuk	שוק
line, row	shura'	שורה
first row	shura' rishona'	שורה ראשונה
shorts	shor'tim	שורטים
root	sho'resh	שורש
partner	shutaf'	שותף
plum	shezif'	שזיף
chess	shakh	שח
black	shakhor'	שחור
swimming	skhiya'	שחיה
arrogant (m.)	shakhtsan'	שחצן
dawn	sha'khar	שחר
flat	shatu'akh	שטוח
foolishness, nonsense	shtut	שטות
nonsense!	shtuyot'!	שטויות!
area	she'takh	שטח
superficial	shitkhi'	שטחי
rug	shati'yakh	שטיח
flood (n.)	shitafon'	שטפון
modernization	shidrug'	שידרוג
balance, equilibrium	shivu'y mishkal'	שיווי משקל
residual	shiyuri'	שיורי
discussion	sikha'	שיחה
method	shita'	שיטה
belonging	shayakh'	שייך
drunk	shikor'	שיכור
let him go	sheyelekh'	שילך
let him go to hell!	sheyelekh' leazazel'!	שילך לעזאזל!
use (n.)	shimush'	שימוש
teeth	shina'im	שיניים
lesson	shiur'	שיעור
hair	sear'	שיער
song	shir	שיר
service	sherut'	שירות
housekeeping	sherut' khadarim'	שירות חדרים
restrooms, bathroom, toilet	shirutim'	שירותים

six	shisha′	שישה
six days	shisha′ yamim′	שישה ימים
sixth	shishi′	שישי
sixty	shishim′	שישים
layer	shikhva′	שכבה
neighborhood	shkhuna′	שכונה
common, frequent	shakhi′yakh	שכיח
neighbor (m.)	shakhen′	שכן
neighbor (f.)	shkhena′	שכנה
of (somebody's)	shel	של
cardiac	shel halev′	של הלב
snow	she′leg	שלג
skeleton	she′led	שלד
his	shelo′	שלו
her	shela′	שלה
peace	shalom′	שלום
hello! good-bye!	shalom′!	שלום!
I'm fine	shlomi′ tov	שלומי טוב
three (f.)	shalosh′	שלוש
three hundred	shlosh meot′	שלוש מאות
thirteen	shlosh′ esre′	שלוש עשרה
three (m.)	shlosha′	שלושה
three days	shlosha yamim′	שלושה ימים
three weeks	shlosha′ shvuot′	שלושה שבועות
thirty	shloshim′	שלושים
three thousand	shlo′shet alafim′	שלושת אלפים
remote control	shalat′	שלט
control, authority	shlita′	שליטה
negative	shlili′	שלילי
one-third	shlish	שליש
my, mine	sheli′	שלי
third	shlishi′	שלישי
your, yours (m.)	shelkha′	שלך
your, yours (f.)	shelakh′	שלך
whole	shalem′	שלם
our, ours	shela′nu	שלנו
the day before yesterday	shilshom′	שלשום
name (n.)	shem	שם
there	sham	שם
left	smol	שמאל
to the left	smo′la	שמאלה
eight	shmona′	שמונה
eighteen	shmona′ asar′	שמונה עשר
eighty	shmonim′	שמונים
rumor (rumors)	shmua′ (shmuot′)	שמועה (שמועות)
happy	same′yakh	שמח
happiness	simkha′	שמחה
my name is	shmi′	שמי
blanket	smikha′	שמיכה

eighth	shmini'	שמיני
hearing	shmia'	שמיעה
dress (n.)	simla'	שמלה
oil	she'men	שמן
fat (adj.) (m.)	shamen'	שמן
fat (adj.) (f.)	shmena'	שמנה
sour cream	shame'net	שמנת
Hear, O Israel!	shma' israel'!	שמע ישראל!
shampoo	shampo'	שמפו
sun	she'mesh	שמש
tooth	shen	שן
hatred	sin"a'	שנאה
year	shana'	שנה
second (m.)	sheni'	שני
second (f.)	shniya'	שניה
second (n.)	shniya'	שניה
two (m.)	shna'im	שניים
twelve (m.)	shneim' asar'	שנים עשר
year 2,000	shnat alpa'im	שנת 2000
annual	shnati'	שנתי
two years	shnata'im	שנתיים
hour	shaa'	שעה
clock, watch (n.)	shaon'	שעון
local time	shaon' mekomi'	שעון מקומי
gate	sha'ar	שער
Jaffa gate	sha'ar ya'fo	שער יפו
Damascus gate	sha'ar shkhem	שער שכם
rate of exchange	sha'ar khalifin'	שער חליפין
language, lip	safa'	שפה
rabbit	shafan'	שפן
abundance	she'fa	שפע
lips	sfata'im	שפתיים
sack	sak	שק
transparent	shakuf'	שקוף
silent	shaket'	שקט
silence, quiet	she'ket	שקט
bag	sakit'	שקית
plug	she'ka	שקע
lie (n.)	she'ker	שקר
liar!	shakran'!	שקרן!
minister	sar	שר
foreign minister	sar hakhuts'	שר החוץ
hot, dry weather	shara'v	שרב
sleeve	sharvul'	שרוול
sixteen	shesh esre'	שש עשרה
shut up!	shtok!	שתוק!
shut up already!	shtok kvar!	שתוק כבר!
drink, beverage	shtiya'	שתיה
two (f.)	shta'im	שתיים
urine	she'ten	שתן

ת

cell	ta	תא
twins	teumim'	תאומים
accident	teuna'	תאונה
road accident	teunat' drakhim'	תאונת דרכים
illumination	teura'	תאורה
theater	teatron'	תאטרון
date	taarikh'	תאריך
exit date	taarikh' yetsia'	תאריך יציאה
entry date	taarikh' knisa'	תאריך כניסה
date of birth	taarikh' leda'	תאריך לידה
grain crops	tvua'	תבואה
intelligence, understanding	tvuna'	תבונה
defeat (n.)	tvusa'	תבוסה
pattern, pan	tavnit'	תבנית
reaction	tguva'	תגובה
strange reaction	tguva' muzara'	תגובה מוזרה
frequent (adj.)	tadir'	תדיר
frequency	tadirut'	תדירות
tea	te	תה
resonance	tehuda'	תהודה
process (n.)	tahalikh'	תהליך
thank you	toda'	תודה
thanks a lot	toda' raba'	תודה רבה
features	tavei' panim'	תוי פנים
contours	tavim'	תוים
content (n.)	to'khen	תוכן
program (computer)	tokhna'	תוכמה
plan (n.), program	tokhnit'	תוכנית
syllabus	tokhnit' limudim'	תוכנית לימודים
supporters	tomkhim'	תומכים
addition, side dish	tose'fet	תוספת
donor	torem'	תורם
inhabitant	toshav'	תושב
nutrition	tzuna'	תזונה
transport	takhbura'	תחבורה
ammunition	takhmo'shet	תחמושת
station	takhana'	תחנה
bus stop	takhanat' o'tobus	תחנת אוטובוס
gasoline station	takhanat' de'lek	תחנת דלק
competition	takharut'	תחרות
bottom	takhtit'	תחתית
gear box	tivat' hilukhim'	תיבת הילוכים
tourist	tayar'	תייר
tourism	tayarut'	תיירות
baby	tinok'	תינוק
bag, handbag	tik	תיק
filing cabinet	tikiya'	תיקיה

corn	ti'ras	תירס
light blue	tkhe'let	תכלת
program	tokhnit'	תכנית
dictation, instructions	takhtiv'	תכתיב
mound (archaeological)	tel	תל
steep	talul'	תלול
innocent	tam	תם
it is over	tam venishlam'	תם ונשלם
picture (n.)	tmuna'	תמונה
always	tamid'	תמיד
support (n.)	tmikha'	תמיכה
naive	tamim'	תמים
honesty, innocence	tmimut'	תמימות
cosmetics	tamrukim'	תמרוקים
road sign	tamrur'	תמרור
stop sign	tamrur' atsor'	תמרור עצור
give	ten	תן
give it to me	ten li oto'	תן לי אותו
let me see	ten li lir"ot'	תן לי לראות
give us (let us)	ten la'nu	תן לנו
Bible	tanakh'	תנ"ך
condition (n.)	tnay	תנאי
necessary condition	tna'y bal yaavor'	תנאי בל יעבור
movement, motion, traffic	tnua'	תנועה
oven	tanur' afiya'	תנור אפיה
certificate	teuda'	תעודה
identity card	teudat' zehut'	תעודת זהות
immigration certificate	teudat' ole'	תעודת עולה
papers (documents), certificates	teudot'	תעודות
canal	taala'	תעלה
razor	ta'ar	תער
exhibition	taarukha'	תערוכה
art exhibition	taarukhat' tsiyurim'	תערוכת ציורים
rate (n.)	taarif'	תעריף
industry	taasiya'	תעשיה
please (Arabic)	tfa'dal	תפדל
oranges	tapuzim'	תפוזים
potato	tapu'akh adama'	תפוח אדמה
apples	tapukhey' ets	תפוחי עץ
stop it!	tafsik'!	תפסיק!
menu	tafrit'	תפריט
fair (n.)	tetsuga'	תצוגה
fashion show	tetsugat' ofna'	תצוגת אופנה
photo	tatslum'	תצלום
fault, failure	takala'	תקלה
record	taklit'	תקליט
socket	te'ka	תקע
an abstract	taktsir'	תקציר

puncture (n.)	te'ker	תקר
press, communications	tiksho'ret	תקשורת
hen	tarnego'let	תרנגלת
crossword, puzzle	tashbets'	תשבץ
answer (n.)	tshuva'	תשובה
desire (n.)	tshuka'	תשוקה
ninth	tshi"i'	תשיעי
payment	tashlum'	תשלום
nine hundred	tsha meot'	תשע מאות
nineteen	tsha' esre'	תשע עשרה
nine	tish"a'	תשעה
ninety	tish"im'	תשעים
tip (n.)	te'sher	תשר
under, sub	tat	תת
very poor level	tat rama'	תת רמה

ENGLISH–HEBREW
DICTIONARY

A

a bit	ktsat′	קצת
a bit more	od ktsat′	עוד קצת
a little	meat′, ktsat	מעט, קצת
a lot	harbe′	הרבה
abdomen	be′ten	בטן
ability	yekho′let	יכולת
able	mesugal′	מסוגל
abortion	hapala′	הפלה
about	al	על
about it	al kakh′	על כך
about what?	al ma?	על מה?
above	meal′, meal′ le...	מעל, מעל ל...
abroad	lekhuts′ laa′rets	לחוץ לארץ
absence	khisaron′	חסרון
absent	khaser′	חסר
absolute	mukhlat′	מוחלט
absolutely not	beferush′ lo	בפרוש לא
absorption	klita′	קליטה
abstract	taktsir′	תקציר
abundance	she′fa	שפע
accelerator	davshat′ gaz	דוושת גז
accept	lekabel′	לקבל
acceptable	mani′yakh et hada′at	מניח את הדעת
accepted	mekubal′, mekube′let	מקובל, מקובלת
accident	teunat′ drakhim′	תאונת דרכים
accompany	lelavot′	ללוות
according to	lefi′, kfi′	לפי, כפי
account	kheshbon′	חשבון
accountant	roe′ kheshbon′	רואה חשבון
acid	khumtsa′	חומצה
across	mee′ver	מעבר
act (n.)	maase′	מעשה
act (v.)	lif′ol′	לפעול
acting	asiya′	עשיה
active	pail′	פעיל
activity	peilut′	פעילות
actually	bae′tsem	בעצם
add	lehosif′	להוסיף
addicted to	makhur′ le...	מכור ל...
addition	tose′fet	תוספת
address (n.)	kto′vet	כתובת
admire	lehaarits′	להעריץ
admit	lehakhnis′	להכניס
adolescent	na′ar	נער

adult (m.)	mevugar'	מבוגר
adult (f.)	mevuge'ret	מבוגרת
adventure	harpatka'	הרפתקה
advertisement	modaa'	מודעה
advice	etsa'	עצה
after	akharey', leakhar', kaavor'	אחרי, לאחר, כעבור
after all	akharey' hakol'	אחרי הכל
after that	akhar' kakh	אחר כך
after this	akharey' ze	אחרי זה
afternoon	tsohora'im	צהריים
afterwards	akhar' kakh	אחר כך
again	shuv	שוב
against	ne'ged	נגד
age	gil	גיל
aggregate	sakh hakol'	סך הכל
agree	lehaskim'	להסכים
agreement	haskama'	הסכמה
aim	matara'	מטרה
air	avir'	אויר
air bag	karit' avir'	כרית אויר
air conditioner	mazgan'	מזגן
air pressure	la'khats avir'	לחץ אויר
airplane	matos'	מטוס
airport	namal' teufa'	נמל תעופה
alert (adj.)	zariz', erani'	זריז, ערני
alive	khay	חי
alkaline	alka'li	אלקלי
all	kol	כל
all around	misaviv'	מסביב
all day	kol hayom'	כל היום
all night	kol halay'la	כל לילה
all the papers (documents)	hamismakhim'	המסמכים
all the time	kol hazman'	כל הזמן
all the way	kol hade'rekh	כל הדרך
allergy	aler'gia	אלרגיה
alliance	brit	ברית
allow	leharshot'	להרשות
allow me	harshe' li	הרשה לי
alone	levad'	לבד
alphabet	a'lef bet	אלף־בית
already	kvar	כבר
also	gam, gam ken	גם, גם כן
alternator	alterna'tor	אלטרנטור
altogether	bikhlal'	בכלל
aluminum	alumi'nium	אלומיניום
always	tamid'	תמיד
ambassador	shagrir'	שגריר
ambulance	ambulan'ce	אמבולנס

ammunition	takhmo'shet	תחמושת
among	beyn	בין
among other things	beyn hasha'ar	בין השאר
amount	skhum	סכום
anchor	o'gen	עוגן
and	ve...	...ו
and even so	uvekhol' zot	ובכל זאת
and so	uvekhen'	ובכן
and that's it!	vetu' lo!	ותו לא!
and what of it?	uma' bekhakh'?	ומה בכך?
angel	mal"akh'	מלאך
anger (n.)	ka'as	כעס
angle	zavit'	זווית
angry	koes'	כועס
animal	khaya'	חיה
ankle	karsul'	קרסול
announce	lehodi'a	להודיע
announcer	kar"yan'	קריין
annual	shnati'	שנתי
another time	pa'am akhe'ret	פעם אחרת
answer (n.)	tshuva'	תשובה
ant (ants)	nemala' (nemalim')	נמלה (נמלים)
antagonism	oyenut'	עוינות
antenna	anten'a	אנטנה
anti-	ne'ged	נגד
antibiotic	antibio'tika	אנטיביאוטיקה
any	kol	כול
anyone	kol ekhad'	כול אחד
anything	kol davar'	כול דבר
anyway	belav' hakhi'	בלוא הכי
aorta	av haorkim'	אב העורקים
apartment	dira'	דירה
apparatus	manganon'	מנגנון
apparently	kfi hanir"e'	כפי הנראה
appetizer	mana' rishona'	מנה ראשונה
apples	tapukhey' ets	תפוחי עץ
application	yisum'	ישום
apply	lifnot'	לפנות
appointment	pgisha'	פגישה
approve	lehaskim' le'	להסכים ל־
April	april'	אפריל
arab	aravi'	ערבי
area	she'takh	שטח
arithmetic	kheshbon'	חשבון
arm	yad	יד
armchair (armchairs)	kursa' (kursaot')	כורסא (כורסאות)
army	tsava'	צבא
army officer	katsin', ktsina'	קצין, קצינה
around	saviv', saviv' le...	סביב, סביב ל...
around the corner	mesaviv' lapina'	מסביב לפינה

arrange	lesader'	לסדר
arrest (n.)	maasar'	מאסר
arrive	lehagi'a	להגיע
arrogant (m.)	shakhtsan'	שחצן
arrogant (f.)	shakhtsanit'	שחצנית
arrow	khets	חץ
art	omanut'	אומנות
art exhibition	taarukhat' tsiyurim'	תערוכת ציורים
article	maamar'	מאמר
artist	tsayar'	צייר
as	kfi she... kmo she...	כפי ש... כמו ש...
as compared to	behashvaa' le	בהשוואה ל...
as long as	kol od	כל עוד
as needed	kfi shetsarikh'	כפי שצריך
as opposed to	leumat'	לאומת
as you know (m.)	kfi sheata' yode'a	כפי שאתה יודע
as you know (f.)	kfi sheat' yoda'at	כפי שאת יודעת
as you please (m.)	eykh sheata' rotse'	איך שאתה רוצה
as you please (f.)	eykh sheat' rotsa'	איך שאת רוצה
aside from	khuts me...	חוץ מ...
ask	lish"ol'	לשאול
asleep	nirdam'	נרדם
assembly	kinus'	כינוס
assimilation	hitbolelut'	התבוללות
at	e'tsel, be...	אצל, ב...
at work	baavoda'	בעבודה
atheist	ateist'	אטיאסט
athletics	atle'tika kala'	אתלטיקה קלה
atmosphere	atmosfi'ra	אטמוספירה
atom	atom'	אטום
attack (n.)	hatkafa'	התקפה
attack (v.)	lehatkif'	להתקיף
attention!	amod' dom!	עמוד דום!
attraction	mshikha'	משיכה
attractive	moshekh', moshe'khet	מושך, מושכת
audience	kahal'	קהל
August	o'gust	אוגוסט
aunt	do'da	דודה
authority	makor' musmakh'	מקור מוסמך
authorization	ishur'	אישור
automatic	otoma'ti	אוטומטי
automation	otoma'tsiya	אוטומציה
autumn	stav	סתו
average	memutsa'	ממוצע
avocado	avoka'do	אבוקדו
awake (adj.)	er	ער
award	tsalash'	צל"ש
away	lo nimtsa'	לא נמצא
awful!	nora'!	נורא!
ax	garzen'	גרזן

axis	tsir	ציר

B

baby	tinok'	תינוק
back	gav	גב
back part	khe'lek akhori'	חלק אחורי
backwards	akho'ra, leakhor'	אחורה, לאחור
bad	ra	רע
bag	tik	תיק
bake	leefot'	לאפות
bakery	maafiya'	מאפיה
balance	shivuy' mishkal'	שיווי משקל
ball	kadur'	כדור
banana (bananas)	bana'na (bana'not)	בננה (בננות)
bandit	shoded'	שודד
bank	bank	בנק
barber	sapar'	ספר
barbershop	maspera'	מספרה
bargain (n.)	mtsia'	מציאה
barley	grisim'	גריסים
barometer	barome'ter	ברומטר
barrier	makhsom'	מחסום
base (n.)	basis'	בסיס
basket	sal	סל
basketball	kadursal'	כדורסל
bastard!	mamzer'!	ממזר!
bath	amba'tiya	אמבטיה
bathing suit	be'ged yam	בגד ים
bathroom	shirutim'	שירותים
battery	solela'	סוללה
battle	krav	קרב
be	lih"yot'	להיות
be careful	lehizaher'	להזהר
be happy	lismo'akh	לשמח
be late	leakher'	לאחר
beach	khof hayam'	חוף הים
beach sandals	naaley' yam	נעלי ים
bead (beads)	kharuz' (kharuzim')	חרוז (חרוזים)
bean (beans)	pul (pulim')	פול (פולים)
beautiful (f.)	yafa'	יפה
beauty (n.)	yo'fi	יופי
because	keyvan' she..., mipney' she...	כיוון ש..., מפני ש...
because of	biglal'	בגלל
because of what?	mipney' ma?	מפני מה?
bed	mita'	מיטה
bedroom	khadar' shena'	חדר שינה
bedspread	kisu'y mita'	כיסוי מיטה
bee	dvora'	דבורה

beer	bi'ra	בירה
beet	se'lek	סלק
beetle	khipushit'	חיפושית
before	lifney'	לפני
before noon	lifney' hatsohora'im	לפני הצהריים
begin	lehatkhil'	להתחיל
beginning	reshit'	ראשית
behavior	hitnahagut'	התנהגות
behind	akharey'	אחרי
behold	harey'	הרי
being that	heyot' ve...	היות ו...
believe	lehaamin'	להאמין
belonging to	shayakh' l...	שייך ל...
beloved	ahuv'	אהוב
below	lema'ta	למטה
belt	khagura'	חגורה
best	hatov' beyoter'	הטוב ביותר
best wishes	kol tuv lekha'	כל טוב לך
Bethlehem	beyt le'khem	בית לחם
between	beyn	בין
beverage	shtiya'	שתיה
Bible	tanakh'	תנ"ך
bicycle	ofana'im	אופניים
big (m.)	gadol'	גדול
big (f.)	gdola'	גדולה
bill (n.)	kheshbon'	חשבון
biology	biolo'gia	ביולוגיה
bird	tsipor'	ציפור
birthday	yom hule'det	יום הלדת
biscuit	biskvit', ugiyot'	בסקוויט, עגיות
bit	tipa'	טיפה
bit more	od ktsat'	עוד קצת
black (m.)	shakhor'	שחור
black (f.)	shkhora'	שחורה
blanket	smikha'	שמיכה
blooper	fash'la	פשלה
blue (m.)	kakhol'	כחול
blue (f.)	kkhula'	כחולה
body	guf	גוף
body lotion	krem guf	קרם גוף
boil (v.)	leharti'yakh	להרתיח
boiling	rote'aykh	רותח
bolt	bari'yakh	בריח
bombing	haftsatsa'	הפצצה
bone	e'tsem	עצם
book (books)	se'fer (sfarim')	ספר (ספרים)
book fair	yarid' sfarim'	יריד ספרים
bookcase	konenit' sfarim'	כוננית ספרים
bookstore	khanut' sfarim'	חנות ספרים
boor	bur	בור

boots	magafa'im	מגפיים
boring	meshaamem'	משעמם
bottle	bakbuk'	בקבוק
bottom	takhtit'	תחתית
boundary	gvul	גבול
bowl (bowls)	keara' (kearot')	קערה (קערות)
box	kufsa'	קופסה
boy	ye'led	ילד
bracelet	tsamid'	צמיד
brakes	blamim'	בלמים
brandy	bran'di	ברנדי
brave (m.)	amits'	אמיץ
brave (f.)	amitsa'	אמיצה
bread	le'khem	לחם
break (n.)	hafsaka'	הפסקה
breakdown in	ke'tser be...	קצר ב...
breakfast	arukhat' bo'ker	ארוחת בוקר
bridge	ge'sher	גשר
bright	bahir'	בהיר
bring	lehavi'	להביא
broad	rakhav'	רחב
broadcaster	kar"yan'	קריין
broken	shavur'	שבור
brought	muva'	מובא
brown (m.)	khum'	חום
brown (f.)	khuma'	חומה
brush (n.)	mivre'shet	מברשת
buffet	miznon'	מזנון
build	livnot'	לבנות
builder	bone'	בונה
building	bin"yan'	בניין
burn (n.)	kviya'	כויה
bus	o'tobus	אוטובוס
bus stop	takhanat' o'tobus	תחנת אוטובוס
business	asakim'	עסקים
busy	asuk'	עסוק
but	aval'	אבל
butcher	itliz'	איטליז
butter	khem"a'	חמאה
buy	liknot'	לקנות
by	al yedey'	על ידי
by chance	bemikre'	במקרה

C

cabbage	kruv	כרוב
cafe	kafe'	קפה
cake	uga'	עוגה
calculated	mekhushav'	מחושב
calculation	khishuv'	חישוב

calculator	makhshevon'	מחשבון
call (v.)	likro' le...	לקרוא ל...
call me	titkasher' elay'	תתקשר אלי
calories	kalo'riyot	קלוריות
camel	gamal'	גמל
camera	matslema'	מצלמה
camp	makhane'	מחנה
camping	kem'ping	קמפינג
can (v.)	yakhol'	יכול
can be	yakhol' lih"yot'	יכול להיות
can not be	lo yakhol' lih"yot'	לא יכול להיות
canal	taala'	תעלה
cancel	levatel'	לבטל
cancellation	bitul'	ביטול
candle	ner	נר
cap	ko'va	כובע
capability	yakho'let	יכולת
capacity	kibo'let	קיבולת
capital	hon	הון
capital city	ir habira'	עיר הבירה
car	mekhonit'	מכונית
card	kartis'	כרטיס
cardboard	karton'	קרטון
cardiac	shel halev'	של הלב
careful (m.)	zahir'	זהיר
careful (f.)	zhira'	זהירה
carefully	bizhirut'	בזהירות
careless (m.)	rashlani'	רשלני
careless (f.)	rashlanit'	רשלנית
cargo	mit"an'	מטען
carpenter	nagar'	נגר
carrot	ge'zer	גזר
cart	agala'	עגלה
cash	mezuman'	מזומן
cashier	kupait'	קופאית
casino	kazi'no	קזינו
cat (cats)	khatul' (khatulim')	חתול (חתולים)
catch (v.)	litpos'	לתפוס
cause	ligrom'	לגרום
cell	ta	תא
cellular phone	pe'lefon	פלאפון
center	merkaz'	מרכז
certain	mesuyam'	מסוים
certain amount	kamut' mesuye'met	כמות מסוימת
certain aspect	tsad mesuyam'	צד מסוים
certain number	mispar' mesuyam'	מספר מסוים
certain type	sug mesuyam'	סוג מסוים
certainly	kamuvan', be'takh	כמובן, בטח
certainly not	behekhlet' lo	בהחלט לא
certificates	mismakhim'	מסמכים

chair (chairs)	kise' (kisaot')	כסא (כסאות)
change (v.)	leshanot'	לשנות
change (n.)	shinuy'	שינוי
change it	teshane' et ze	תשנה את זה
change (money)	o'def	עודף
change point (*bank*)	khalfan' ksafim'	חלפן כספים
character	o'fi	אופי
cheap	zol	זול
check (v.)	livdok'	לבדוק
checkbook	pinkas' tche'kim	פנקס שקים
checking	bdika'	בדיקה
cheese	gvina'	גבינה
chemist	kimai'	כימאי
chemistry	ki'miya	כימיה
chess	shakh	שח
chest	khaze'	חזה
chicken	of	עוף
chief	rashi'	ראשי
chief engineer	mehandes' rashi'	מהנדס ראשי
children	yeladim'	ילדים
children's diseases	makhalot' yeladim'	מחלות ילדים
choose	livkhor'	לבחור
Church of the Holy Sepulchre	knesiyat' hake'ver	כנסיית הקבר
cinnamon	kinamon'	קנמון
circle	igul'	עיגול
circus	kirkas'	קרקס
city	ir	עיר
civics	ezrakhut'	אזרחות
civil	ezrakhi'	אזרחי
clarify	lehav"hir'	להבהיר
class	kita'	כיתה
classification	miyun'	מיון
classroom	kita'	כיתה
clay	khemar'	חמר
clean (m.)	naki'	נקי
clean (f.)	nekiya'	נקיה
clear	meelav'	מובן מאליו
clearly	barur'	ברור
clerk (m.)	pakid'	פקיד
clerk (f.)	pkida'	פקידה
climate	aklim'	אקלים
climb	letapes'	לטפס
clinic	kupat' kholim'	קופת חולים
clock	shaon'	שעון
close the gap	lisgor' et hapa'ar	לסגור את הפער
closed (f.)	sagur'	סגור
closed (m.)	sgura'	סגורה
closet	aron	ארון
closing	sgira'	סגירה

clothes	bgadim'	בגדים
clothes closet	aron' bgadim'	ארון בגדים
cloud (clouds)	anan' (ananim')	ענן (עננים)
clutch	klyach', matsmed'	קלאץ', מצמד
coach	me'amen'	מאמן
coarse	gas, gas ru'akh	גס, גס רוח
coast	khof	חוף
coat	meil'	מעיל
coffee	kafe'	קפה
coffeeshop	beyt kafe'	בית קפה
cognac	ko'n"yak	קוניק
coin	matbe'a	מטבע
cold	kar	קר
cold water	ma'im karim'	מים קרים
color	tse'va	צבע
column	amud'	עמוד
comb	masrek'	מסרק
come	lavo'	לבוא
come back	lakhzor'	לחזור
come here	bo he'na	בוא הנה
come in!	na lehikanes'	נא להכנס
come on	ha'va	הבה
come to	bo'u el	בואו אל
commercial	miskhari'	מסחרי
common	shakhi'yakh	שכיח
common market	hashuk' hameshutaf'	השוק המשותף
commotion	saarat' rukhot'	סערת רוחות
communications	tiksho'ret	תקשורת
community	kehila'	קהלה
compass	matspen'	מצפן
completely	legam'rey	לגמרי
completely incidental	shuli' legam're	שולי לגמרי
compression	dkhisa'	דחיסה
comprised of	murkav' mi...	מורכב מ...
computer	makhshev'	מחשב
concentration	rikuz'	ריכוז
concerning	benoge'a le"...	בנוגע ל...
concerning which	benoge'a lekhakh'	בנוגע לכך
concert	kontsert'	קונצרט
conduction	holakha'	הולכה
confirm	leasher'	לאשר
conflict	imut'	עימות
confusion	bilbul'	בלבול
congratulations	kol hakavod', birkotay'	כל הכבוד, ברכותי
connection	khibur', ke'sher	חיבור, קשר
consider	lishkol'	לשקול
considering that	mitkhashev' be...	מתחשב ב...
construction	bin"yan'	בנין

construction worker	poel' bin"yan'	פועל בנין
consumption	tsrikha'	צריכה
contact (n.)	maga'	מגע
continue	lehamshikh'	להמשיך
contours	tavim'	תוים
contraction	hitkavtsut'	התכווצות
contradicts himself	soter' et atsmo'	סותר את עצמו
contributions	ezra' kaspit', trumot'	עזרה כספית, תרומות
controller	mevaker'	מבקר
conventional sign	siman' mekubal'	סימן מקובל
conversation	sikha'	שיחה
conversion	hamara'	המרה
cook (n.)	tabakh'	טבח
cook (v.)	levashel'	לבשל
cooked	mevushal'	מבושל
cookies	ugiyot'	עוגיות
cooking	bishul'	בישול
cool (adj.)	karir'	קריר
coordinate	letaem'	לתאם
copper	nekho'shet	נחושת
coral	almog'	אלמוג
corn	ti'ras	תירס
corner	pina'	פינה
corner shop	mako'let	מכולת
correct (adj.)	nakhon'	נכון
correctly	nakhon'	נכון
correspondence	hitkatvut'	התכתבות
correspondent	katav'	כתב
cosmetics	tamrukim'	תמרוקים
cost (n.)	alut'	עלות
cost (v.)	laalot'	לעלות
cost him a lot	ala' lo beyo'ker	עלה לו ביוקר
cottage	bayt katan'	בית קטן
cotton	kutna'	כותנה
could be	yakhol' lih"yot'	יכול להיות
count (n.)	kheshbon'	חשבון
count (v.)	lispor'	לספור
countdown	sfira' leakhor'	ספירה לאחור
counter-clockwise	ne'ged kivun' hashaon'	נגד כיוון השעון
counting	sfira'	ספירה
country	e'rets	ארץ
court *(law)*	beyt mishpat'	בית משפט
court *(sport)*	migrash' sport	מגרש ספורט
cover	kisu'y	כיסוי
cow (cows)	para' (parot')	פרה (פרות)
critical	kri'ti	קריטי
cross (v.)	laavor'	לעבור
crossroad	tso'met	צומת

cry (v.)	livkot'	לבכות
crystal	bdo'lakh	בדולח
cucumber	melafefon'	מלפפון
cup	kos	כוס
current n	ze'rem	זרם
current (electric)	ze'rem khashmali'	זרם חשמלי
curriculum vitae	korot' khaim'	קורות חיים
curtain	vilon'	וילון
curve (n.)	akuma'	עקומה
customs	me'khes	מכס
cut (v.)	khatakh'	חתך
cute (adj.), (m.)	khamud'	חמוד
cute (adj.), (f.)	khamuda'	חמודה
cute (n.), (m.)	khatikh'	חתיך
cute (n.), (f.)	khatikha'	חתיכה
cycle (n.)	makhzor'	מחזור

D

dairy (n.)	makhleva'	מחלבה
dairy (milk product)	khalavi '	חלבי
Damascus Gate	sha'ar shkhem	שער שכם
dance (n.)	rikud'	ריקוד
dance (v.)	lirkod'	לרקוד
dancing	rikudim'	ריקודים
danger	sakana'	סכנה
dangerous	mesukan'	מסוכן
dark	kho'shekh	חושך
date	taarikh'	תאריך
date of birth	taarikh' leda'	תאריך לידה
daughter	bat	בת
dawn	sha'khar	שחר
day	yom	יום
Dead Sea	yam hame'lakh	ים המלח
death	ma'vet	מוות
December	detsem'ber	דצמבר
decision	hakhlata'	החלטה
decision-making	kabalat' hakhlata'	קבלת החלטה
decline (n.)	yerida'	ירידה
decrease (n.)	horada'	הורדה
decrease (v.)	lare'det	לרדת
deed	maase'	מעשה
deep (m.)	amok'	עמוק
deep (f.)	amuka'	עמוקה
defeat (n.)	tvusa'	תבוסה
defect (n.)	pgam'	פגם
defense	hagana'	הגנה
definitely	behekhlet'	בהחלט
definitely not!	beshum' panim' veo'fen	בשום פנים ואופן

definition	hagdara'	הגדרה
deflection	stiya'	סטייה
degree	maala'	מעלה
delay (n.)	ikuv'	עיכוב
delay (v.)	leakev'	לעכב
demand(s) (m.)	doresh'	דורש
demand(s) (f.)	dore'shet	דורשת
demonstration	hafgana'	הפגנה
density	tsfifut'	צפיפות
dental	shel shina'im	של שיניים
dentist	rofe' shina'im	רופא שיניים
deportation of refugees	gerush' plitim'	גירוש פליטים
deposit (n.)	pikadon'	פיקדון
deposit (v.)	lehafkid'	להפקיד
depth	o'mek	עומק
describe	letaer'	לתאר
desert (n.)	midbar'	מדבר
desirable	ratsu'y	רצוי
desire (n.)	tshuka'	תשוקה
despite	af al pi she...	אף על פי ש...
despondent (m.)	meyuash'	מיואש
despondent (f.)	meyue'shet	מיואשת
destroy	leharos'	להרוס
determination	nekhishut'	נחישות
development	pitu'akh	פיתוח
deviation	stiya'	סטייה
dew	tal	טל
diagonal	alakhson'	אלכסון
dial (v.)	lekhayeg'	לחייג
diameter	ko'ter	קוטר
diamond	yahalom'	יהלום
dictate	lehakhtiv'	להכתיב
dictated (m.)	mukhtav'	מוכתב
dictation	takhtiv'	תכתיב
dictionary	milon'	מילון
die	lamut'	למות
diet	die'ta	דיאטה
difference	sho'ni	שוני
different	shone'	שונה
difficult	kashe'	קשה
difficulty	ko'shi	קושי
digit	sifra'	ספרה
dine	lis"od'	לסעוד
dinner	arukhat' e'rev	ארוחת ערב
direct (adj.)	yashir'	ישיר
direct current	ze'rem kavu'a	זרם קבוע
direction	kivun'	כיוון
director	menahel'	מנהל
dirty (m.)	melukhlakh'	מלוכלך

dirty (f.)	melukhle'khet	מלוכלכת
disappear	lehialem'	להיעלם
disappointed (m.)	meukhzav'	מאוכזב
disappointed (f.)	meukhze'vet	מאוכזבת
disconnection	ne'tek	נתק
discotheque	diskotek'	דיסקוטק
discussion	sikha'	שיחה
disgusting	mag''il'	מגעיל
dish	tsala'khat	צלחת
distance	mirkhak'	מרחק
distribution	khaluka'	חלוקה
divided	mekhulak'	מחולק
divorce	gerushin'	גירושין
do	laasot'	לעשות
do you?	haim'?	האם?
do you care?	ikhpat' lekha'?, lakh	איכפת לך?, לך
do you hear?	shome'a?, shoma'at	שומע?, שומעת
doctor	rofe'	רופא
document	teuda'	תעודה
documents	mismakhim', teudot'	מסמכים, תעודות
does?	haim?	האם?
does it open?	ze niftakh'?	זה נפתח?
dog (dogs)	ke'lev (klavim')	כלב (כלבים)
dollar	dolar'	דולר
done	asu'y	עשוי
donkey	khamor'	חמור
donor	torem'	תורם
don't	al	אל
don't be afraid!	al tefakhed'!	אל תפחד!
don't be like that!	al tihye' kaze'!	אל תהיה כזה!
don't bother!	lo tsarikh'!	לא צריך!
don't bother me!	red mime'ni!	רד ממני!
don't do that!	al taase' zot!	אל תעשה זאת!
don't forget!	al tishkakh'!	אל תשכח!
don't take!	al tikakh'!	אל תקח!
don't worry!	al tid''ag'!	אל תדאג!
don't you dare!	oy' veavoy' lekha'!	אוי ואבוי לך!
door	de'let	דלת
double	kaful'	כפול
down	lema'ta	למטה
draw (v.)	letsayet', lesartet'	לצייר, לסרטט
drawing	tsiyur', sirtut'	ציור, שרטוט
dress (n.)	simla'	שמלה
drill	makdekha'	מקדחה
drill bit	makde'yakh	מקדח
drink (v.)	lishtot'	לשתות
drink (n.)	shtiya'	שתיה
drink a lot	lishtot' harbe'	לשתות הרבה
drinking water	mey shtiya'	מי שתיה
drive (n.)	nehiga'	נהיגה

drive (v.)	linhog'	לנהוג
driver	nahag'	נהג
driver's license	rishyon' nehiga'	רשיון נהיגה
dry (adj.)	yavesh'	יבש
dry (v.)	leyabesh'	ליבש
duck (n.)	barvaz'	ברווז
during	beme'shekh	במשך
during the day	bayom'	ביום
during the trip	beme'shekh hanesiya'	במשך הנסיעה
dust	avak'	אבק
duty	hitkhayvut'	התחייבות

E

each	kol ekhad'	כל אחד
ear	o'zen	אוזן
early	mukdam'	מוקדם
earthquake	reidat' adama'	רעידת אדמה
east	mizrakh'	מזרח
easy	kal	קל
eat	leekhol'	לאכול
eating	akhila'	אכילה
echo (n.)	hed	הד
economy	kalkala'	כלכלה
education	khinukh'	חינוך
effect (n.)	ro'shem	רושם
efficiency	yailut'	יעילות
efficient	yail'	יעיל
egg	beytsa'	ביצה
eggplant	khatsilim'	חצילים
Egypt	mitsra'im	מצרים
eight	shmona'	שמונה
eighteen	shmona' asar'	שמונה עשר
eighth	shmini'	שמיני
eighty	shmonim'	שמונים
Eilat	eylat'	אילת
elbow	marpek'	מרפק
elder	mevugar' yoter'	מבוגר יותר
electric	khashmali'	חשמלי
electrical	khashmali'	חשמלי
electrical appliances	makhshirey' khashmal'	מכשירי חשמל
electrical outlet	nekudat' khashmal'	נקודת חשמל
electrician	khashmalay'	חשמלאי
electricity	khashmal'	חשמל
electronics	elektro'nika	אלקטרוניקה
elevator	maalit'	מעלית
eleven	akhad' asar	אחד עשר
embitterment	hitmarmerut	התמרמרות
emergency exit	yetsiat' kherum'	יציאת חרום

emergency medical unit	magen' david' adom'	מגן דוד אדום
emigration	yerida'	ירידה
emission	plita'	פליטה
empty	reyk	ריק
encountered difficulties	nitkal' bekshaim'	נתקל בקשיים
end (n.)	sof	סוף
endurance	svilut'	סבילות
enemy	oyev'	אויב
engine	mano'a	מנוע
engineer	mehandes'	מהנדס
engineering	handasa'	הנדסה
enjoy	lehenot'	להנות
enlistment orders	tsav giyus'	צו גיוס
enough	maspik'	מספיק
enter	lehikanes'	להיכנס
enter! come in!	yavo'!	יבוא!
entered	nikhnas'	ניכנס
entirely	legam'rey	לגמרי
entrance	knisa'	כניסה
entrance, opening	pe'takh	פתח
entry	knisa'	כניסה
entry date	taarikh' knisa'	תאריך כניסה
envelope	maatafa'	מעטפה
environment	sviva'	סביבה
equal (m.)	shave'	שווה
equal (f.)	shava'	שווה
equality	shiv"yon'	שיוויון
equation	mishvaa'	משוואה
equilibrium	shivu'y mishkal'	שיווי משקל
equipment	tsiyud'	ציוד
escape (n.)	brikha'	בריחה
escape (v.)	lehimalet'	להמלט
especially	bimyukhad'	במיוחד
evaluate	lehaarikh'	להעריך
even	afi'lu	אפילו
even more so	al akhat' ka'ma vekha'ma	על אחת כמה וכמה
evening	e'rev	ערב
every	kol	כל
every single one	ekhad' ekhad'	אחד אחד
everybody is busy	kulam' asukim'	כולם עסוקים
everyone	kol ekhad'	כל אחד
everyone went out	kulam' yatsu'	כולם יצאו
everything	hakol'	הכל
everything is fine	hakol' bese'der	הכל בסדר
everything is lost	hakol' avud'	הכל אבוד
everything is o.k.	hakol' bese'der	הכל בסדר
evident	muvan' meelav'	מובן מאליו

exactly	bediyuk'	בדיוק
exactly on time	bediyuk' bazman'	בדיוק בזמן
exam	bkhina'	בחינה
examine	livdok'	לבדוק
excellent	metsuyan'	מצויין
excellent service	sherut' meule'	שרות מעולה
excellently	metsuyan'	מצוין
except for	khuts mi..., prat le...	חוץ מ..., פרט ל...
except for me	khuts mime'ni	חוץ ממני
except for that	prat lekhakh'	פרט לכך
excitement	hitragshut'	התרגשות
exciting	meragesh	מרגש
excursion	tiyul'	טיול
excuse me!	slikha'!	סליחה!
exercise	hit"amlut'	התעמלות
exhibition	taarukha'	תערוכה
existence	kiyum'	קיום
exit (n.)	yetsiya'	יציאה
exit (v.)	latset'	לצאת
exit date	taarikh' yetsiya'	תאריך יציאה
expansion	hitpashtut'	התפשטות
expectation	tsipiya'	ציפיה
expensive	ya'kar	יקר
expired	pag to'kef	פג תוקף
explain	lehasbir'	להסביר
explanation	hesber'	הסבר
explicitly	beferush'	בפרוש
export (n.)	yetsu'	יצוא
export (v.)	leyatse'	ליצא
exposition	yarid'	יריד
external (m.)	khitsoni'	חיצוני
external (f.)	khitsonit'	חיצונית
eye	a'yin	עין

F

face (n.)	panim'	פנים
fact	uvda'	עובדה
factory	mif"al'	מפעל
fainting	mit"alef'	מתעלף
fair (n.)	tetsuga', yarid'	תצוגה, יריד
fall, autumn	stav	סתיו
fall (v.)	lipol'	ליפול
fall (n.)	nefila'	נפילה
family	mishpakha'	משפחה
fan	meavrer'	מאוורר
far	rakhok'	רחוק
farm	meshek'	משק
farmer	ikar'	איכר
farther	ha'l"a	הלאה

fashion show	tetsugat' ofna'	תצוגת אופנה
fast	maher'	מהר
fat (adj.), (m.)	shamen'	שמן
fat (adj.), (f.)	shmena'	שמנה
fat (n.)	shoman'	שומן
father	a'ba	אבא
favor	tova'	טובה
features (facial)	tavey' panim'	תוי פנים
February	fe'bruar	פברואר
feel (n.)	hargasha'	הרגשה
feel (v.)	lehargish'	להרגיש
feels (f.)	margish'	מרגיש
feels (m.)	margisha'	מרגישה
feet	ragla'im	רגליים
fellow	bakhur'	בחור
female	nekeva'	נקבה
few, a few	meat'	מעט
fiber (fibers)	siv (sivim')	סיב (סיבים)
fictitious story	sipur' badu'y	ספור בדוי
field	sade'	שדה
fifteen	khamisha' asar'	חמישה עשר
fifteenth	khe'lek hakhamisha' asar'	חלק החמישה עשר
fifth	khamishi'	חמישי
fifty	khamishim'	חמישים
fight (n.)	maavak'	מאבק
fight (v.)	lehilakhem'	להלחם
figure	sifra'	ספרה
film	se'ret	סרט
finally	sof sof	סוף סוף
financial assistance	ezra' kaspit', trumot'	עזרה כספית, תרומות
find	limtso'	למצוא
find out	levarer'	לברר
fine (penalty)	knas	קנס
finish (v.)	ligmor'	לגמור
finish (n.)	gmar	גמר
finishes (m.)	gomer'	גומר
finishes (f.)	gome'ret	גומרת
fire	esh	אש
first	rishon'	ראשון
first and foremost	berosh' uverishona'	בראש ובראשונה
first of all	ko'dem kol	קודם כל
first row	shura' rishona'	שורה ראשונה
fish (fish)	dag (dagim')	דג (דגים)
five	khamisha'	חמישה
flag	de'gel	דגל
flame	lehava'	להבה
flat	shatu'akh	שטוח
flight	tisa'	טיסה

flight arrival	nekhita'	נחיתה
flight departure	tisa' yotset'	טיסה יוצאת
flood (n.)	shitafon'	שטפון
floor	ritspa'	רצפה
flower (flowers)	perakh' (prakhim')	פרח (פרחים)
fly (v.)	latus'	לטוס
fly (flies)	zvuv (zvuvim')	זבוב (זבובים)
focus	moked'	מוקד
food	o'khel	אוכל
food processor	meabed' mazon'	מעבד מזון
fool	tipesh'	טיפש
foot	re'gel	רגל
football	kadure'gel	כדורגל
for	bead', bishvil'	בעד, בשביל
for a certain time	lezman' mesuyam'	לזמן מסוים
for a few minutes	lekha'ma dakot'	לכמה דקות
for a long time	harbe' zman	הרבה זמן
for a while	ktsat	קצת
for all this	al kol panim'	על כל פנים
for half an hour	lekhatsi' shaa'	לחצי שעה
for it, about it	al kakh	על כך
for me	bishvili'	בשבילי
for nothing	lashav'	לשווא
for sure	kamuvan', be'takh	כמובן, בטח
for ten minutes	lee'ser dakot'	לעשר דקות
for that reason	leshem' kakh	לשם כך
for the bus	lao'tobus	לאוטובוס
for the meeting	lapgisha'	לפגישה
for the movie	lase'ret	לסרט
for the plane	lamatos'	למטוס
for the show	lehatsaga'	להצגה
for the train	lerake'vet	לרכבת
for, in order to	biglal' she...	בגלל ש...
forbidden!	asur'!	אסור!
force (n.)	ko'akh	כוח
forehead	me'tsakh	מצח
foreign	zar	זר
Foreign Minister	sar hakhuz'	שר החוץ
foresight	reiya' mefuka'khat	ראיה מפוקחת
forever	leolam'	לעולם
forget it!	azov' et ze!	עזוב את זה!
forgive me	slakh' li	סלח לי
fork (forks)	mazleg' (mazlegot')	מזלג (מזלגות)
form (n.)	to'fes	טופס
forty	arbaim'	ארבעים
forward	kadi'ma	קדימה
four	arbaa'	ארבעה
four days	arbaa' yamim'	ארבעה ימים
fourteen	arbaa' asar'	ארבעה עשר
fourth	revii'	רביעי

frame	misge'ret	מסגרת
frankfurter	naknikiya'	נקניקיה
free (adj.)	khinam', bekhinam'	חינם, בחינם
freedom	kherut'	חירות
freeze	lehakpi'	להקפיא
French fries	tchips	ציפס
frequency	tadirut'	תדירות
frequent	shakhiyakh'	שכיח
fresh (m.)	tari'	טרי
fresh (f.)	triya'	טריה
Friday	yom shishi'	יום שישי
fried egg	khavita'	חביתה
friend (friends)	khaver' (khaverim')	חבר (חברים)
from	min, me...	מן, מ...
from a distance	merakhok'	מרחוק
from above	milema'la	מלמעלה
from all this	mikol' ze	מכל זה
from below	milema'ta	מלמטה
from everything	mikol' hainyanim'	מכל הענינים
from here	mikan'	מכאן
from school	mebeyt' hase'fer	מבית הספר
from the building	mehabin"yan'	מהבנין
from the chair	mehakise'	מהכיסא
from the evening	mehae'rev	מהערב
from the house	mehaba'it	מהבית
from the morning	mehabo'ker	מהבוקר
from the stairs	mehamadregot'	מהמדרגות
from the table	mehashulkhan'	מהשולחן
from then	meaz'	מאז
from there	misham'	משם
from under	mita'khat le...	מתחת ל...
from what?	mima'?	ממה?
from where?	meey'fo?	מאיפה?
from work	meavoda'	מעבודה
front	khazit'	חזית
fruit	pri'	פרי
fruit trees	atsey' pri	עצי פרי
fry	letagen'	לטגן
frying pan	makhvat' (makhvatot')	מחבת (מחבתות)
fuel	de'lek	דלק
full (adj.)	male'	מלא
full board	hakol' male'	הבול מלא
fun	keif	כיף
furniture	rehitim'	רהיטים
fuse	pkak	פקק
future	atid'	עתיד

G

Galilee	galil'	גליל
game	miskhak'	משחק
gap	pa'ar	פער
garage	mosakh'	מוסך
garbage	ashpa'	אשפה
garden	gina'	גינה
gas	gaz	גז
gasoline	de'lek	דלק
gasoline station	takhanat' de'lek	תחנת דלק
gate	sha'ar	שער
gear box	tevat' hilukhim'	תיבת הילוכים
generous (m.)	nadiv'	נדיב
generous (f.)	nediva'	נדיבה
geography	geogra'fia	גיאוגרפיה
get	lehasig', lekabel'	להסיג, לקבל
get in touch	lehitkasher'	להתקשר
get out	tse	צא
get out of here!	tse mikan'!	צא מכאן!
get up!	kum!	קום!
get up already!	kum kvar!	קום כבר!
girl	bakhura'	בחורה
give (v.)	latet'	לתת
give it to me	ten li oto'	תן לי אותו
give us (let us)	ten la'nu	תן לנו
gives (m.)	noten'	נותן
gives (f.)	note'net	נותנת
gladly	beratson'	ברצון
glass	zkhukhit'	זכוכית
glove	kfafa'	כפפה
glue	de'vek	דבק
go	lale'khet	ללכת
goes (m.)	holekh'	הולך
goes (f.)	hole'khet	הולכת
go already!	lekh' kvar!	לך כבר!
go back	lakhzor' bekhazara'	לחזור בחזרה
go out	latset'	לצאת
goat	ez	עז
God	elokim', hashem'	אלקים, השם
God forbid!	khas veshalom'!	חס ושלום!
God willing!	beezrat' hashem'!	בעזרת השם!
gold	zahav'	זהב
golf	golf	גולף
good	tov	טוב
good luck	kol tuv lekha'	כל טוב לך
good morning	bo'ker tov	בוקר טוב
good news	yedia' mesama'khat	ידיעה משמחת
good night	lay'la tov	לילה טוב
good-looking (m.)	yafe'	יפה
good-looking (f.)	yafa'	יפה

good-bye	shalom′	שלום
goods	skhura′	סחורה
got screwed	nidfak′	נדפק
government	mimshala′	ממשלה
government spokesperson	dover′ hamimshala′	דובר הממשלה
gradually	behadraga′	בהדרגה
grain crops	tvua′	תבואה
granddaughter	nekhda′	נכדה
grandfather	sa′ba	סבה
grandmother	sa′vta	סבתא
grandson	ne′khed	נכד
grape harvest	batsir′	בציר
grapefruit (grapefruits)	eshkolit′ (eshkoliyot′)	אשכולית (אשכוליות)
grapes	anavim′	ענבים
grass	de′she	דשא
grave (m.)	khamur′	חמור
grave (f.)	khamura′	חמורה
gray (m.)	afor′	אפור
gray (f.)	afora′	אפורה
grease	griz	גריז
great!	yesh!	יש!
great	nehedar′, yo′fi	נהדר, יופי
great evening	e′rev nehedar′	ערב נהדר
great majority	rov makhri′a	רוב מכריע
green (m.)	yarok′	ירוק
green (f.)	yeruka′	ירוקה
green field	sade′ yarok′	שדה ירוק
greengrocer	yarkan′	ירקן
greenish	yarakrak′	ירקרק
grid	re′shet	רשת
grill	al haesh′	על האש
grinder	mashkhe′zet	משחזת
grocery	mako′let	מכלת
group	kvutsa′	קבוצה
grow (v.)	ligdol′	לגדול
growing gap	pa′ar holekh′ vegadel′	פער הולך וגדל
growth	tsmikha′	צמיחה
guess	lenakhesh′	לנחש
guide (m.)	madrikh′	מדריך
guide (f.)	madrikha′	מדריכה
gun	ekdakh′	אקדח
gym	hit″amlut′	התעמלות

H

habit	hergel′	הרגל
hair	sear′	שיער
half	khetsi′, makhatsit′	חצי, מחצית

half a kilogram	khatsi' ki'lo	חצי קילו
hammer	patish'	פטיש
hand	yad	יד
handbag	tik	תיק
handle	yadit'	ידית
hands	yada'im	ידיים
handsome	khatikh'	חתיך
handwriting	ktav yad	כתב יד
happen	likrot'	לקרות
happen to	lehizdamen'	להזדמן
happiness	simkha'	שמחה
happy	same'yakh	שמח
hard	kashe'	קשה
hard times	zmanim' kashim'	זמנים קשים
hard to know	kashe' lada'at	קשה לדעת
hard to understand	kashe lehavin'	קשה להבין
hardly	beko'shi	בקושי
harvest	katif'	קטיף
hastily	bekhipazon'	בחיפזון
hat	ko'va	כובע
hatred	sin"a'	שנאה
have	yesh	יש
have a nice time	bilu'y naim'	בלוי נעים
he	hu	הוא
(he) has	yesh lo	יש לו
he looks	hu nir"e'	הוא נראה
(he) was able	ala' beyadav'	עלה בידיו
head	rosh	ראש
head covering	kisuy' rosh	כיסוי ראש
headaches	keevey' rosh	כאבי ראש
healthy (m.)	bari'	בריא
healthy (f.)	bria'	בריאה
hear	lishmo'a	לשמוע
Hear, O Israel!	shma' israel'!	שמע ישראל
hearing	shmia'	שמיעה
hears (m.)	shome'a	שומע
hears (f.)	shoma'at	שומעת
heart	lev	לב
heart diseases	makhalot' lev	מחלות לב
heating	hasaka'	הסקה
heavy	kaved'	כבד
heavy burden	ne'tel kaved'	נטל כבד
heel	akev'	עקב
height	go'va	גובה
hello! good-bye!	shalom'!	שלום!
help (n.)	ezra'	עזרה
help (v.)	laazor'	לעזור
help me, please	taazor' li bevakasha'	תעזור לי בבקשה
helping	matan' ezra'	מתן עזרה
hen	tarnego'let	תרנגלת

her	ota'	אותה
here	po, kan	פה, כאן
here is	yesh kan	יש כאן
here it is written	kan katuv'	כאן כתוב
hi!	a'halan!	אהלן!
hide	lehitkhabe'	להתחבא
high	gavo'a	גבוה
high humidity	lakhut' gvoha'	לחות גבוהה
high jump	kfitsa' lago'va	קפיצה לגובה
high pressure	la'khats gavo'a	לחץ גבוה
high temperature	khom gavo'ha	חום גבוה
hike (n.)	tiyul'	טיול
hill	giv"a'	גבעה
him	oto'	אותו
hintingly	bere'mez	ברמז
his	shelo'	שלו
history	histo'ria	הסטוריה
hit (n.)	pgia'	פגיעה
hold (v.)	lehakhzik'	להחזיק
hole	khor	חור
holiday	khag	חג
home (direction)	habay'ta	הביתה
home	habayt'	הבית
honestly	bakenut'	בכנות
honey	dvash	דבש
horrible	zvaa'	זוועה
horse (horses)	sus' (susim')	סוס (סוסים)
hospital	beit kholim'	בית חולים
hot	kham	חם
hot water	ma'im khamim'	מים חמים
hotel	malon'	מלון
hour	shaa'	שעה
house	ba'yt	בית
housekeeping	sherut' khadarim'	שירות חדרים
how?	eykh?	איך?
how are things?	ma nishma'?	מה נשמע?
how are you?	ma shlomkha'?	מה שלומך?
how much?	ka'ma?	כמה?
human	adam'	אדם
human rights	zkhuyot' adam'	זכויות אדם
humanity	tse'lem enosh'	צלם אנוש
hundred	me'a	מאה
hundredth	meit'	מאית
hunger (n.)	ra'av	רעב
hungry	raev'	רעב
hypocrite!	tsavu'a!	צבוע!

I

I	ani'	אני

I'm afraid	ani' mefakhed'	אני מפחד
I'm fine	shlomi' tov	שלומי טוב
I ask for	ani' mevakesh'	אני מבקש
I beg your pardon	tislakh' li bevakasha'	תסלח לי בבקשה
I called you	kara'ti lekha'	קראתי לך
I didn't know	lo yada'ti	לא ידעתי
I don't care	ze lo meziz' li	זה לא מזיז לי
I don't remember	eyne'ni zokher'	אינני זוכר
I don't want to!	lo rotse'	לא רוצה
I doubt	yesh li safek'	יש לי ספק
I forgot	shakhakh'ti	שכחתי
I need	ani' tsarikh'	אני צריך
I want	ani' rotse'	אני רוצה
I want to ask	ani rotse' lish"ol'	אני רוצה לשאול
I want to buy	ani' rotse' liknot'	אני רוצה לקנות
I'll check it	evdok' zot	אבדוק זאת
ice	ke'rakh	קרח
ice cream	gli'da	גלידה
idea	raayon'	רעיון
identity card	teudat' zehut'	תעודת זהות
idiot!	tum'tum! tem'bel!	טומטום! טמבל!
if	im	אם
if so	im kakh	אם כך
illumination	teura'	תאורה
immediately	miyad'	מיד
immigration certificate	teudat' ole'	תעודת עולה
impact	hashpaa'	השפעה
importance	khashivut'	חשיבות
important	khashuv'	חשוב
imported	muva'	מובא
impossible!	i-efshar'!	אי אפשר!
imprecise	lo meduyak'	לא מדויק
impulse	da'khaf	דחף
impulsively	bifzizut'	בפזיזות
in	be...	ב...
in a drawer	bamegira'	במגירה
in a hospital	beveit' kholim'	בבית חולים
in a lab	bemaabada'	במעבדה
in a while	beod' zman ma	בעוד זמן מה
in accordance with	behet"em' le...	בהתאם ל...
in all the details	bekhol' hapratim'	בכל הפרטים
in any case	beyn ko vakho'	בין כה וכה
in bed	bamita'	במיטה
in demand	nidrash'	נדרש
in front of	lifney'	לפני...
in general	bikhlal'	בכלל
in grief	betsaar'	בצער
in his room	bakhe'der shelo'	בחדר שלו
in light of	leor'	לאור

English	Transliteration	Hebrew
in order to	bishvil, bikhdey'	בשביל, בכדי
in short	bekitsur'	בקיצור
in the beginning	bahatkhala'	בהתחלה
in the distance	bamerkhak'	במרחק
in the end	sofo' shel davar'	סופו של דבר
	haya' she...	היה ש...
in the evening	bae'rev	בערב
in the exchange rate	beshaa'r hamatbe'a	בשער המטבע
in the handbag	batik'	בטיק
in the long run	bitvakh' arokh'	בטווח ארוך
in the morning	babo'ker	בבוקר
in the office	bamisrad'	במשרד
in the short run	bitvakh' katsar'	בטווח קצר
in this matter	bainyan' haze'	בענין הזה
in vain	lashav'	לשווא
incorrect	lo nakhon'	לא נכון
incorrectly	lo nakhon'	לא נכון
increase (n.)	aliya'	עליה
increase (v.)	lehagdil'	להגדיל
indeed	akhen'	אכן
independence	atsmaut'	עצמאות
independent	atsmai'	עצמאי
indicate	lesamen'	לסמן
indicator lights	vin'kerim	וינקרים
indirectly	beakifin'	בעקיפין
induction *(elec.)*	hashraa'	השראה
industry	taasiya'	תעשיה
inexpensive	zol	זול
infection	zihum'	זיהום
infectious diseases	makhalot' medabkot'	מחלות מדבקות
information	meyda'	מידע
information (office)	modiin'	מודעין
inhabitant	toshav'	תושב
inhabited	meyushav'	מיושב
ink	d"yo	דיו
inn	pundak'	פונדק
inner tube	pnimit'	פנימית
innocent	khaf mipe'sha	חף מפשע
inside	bifnim', betokh'	בפנים, בתוך
instant (m.)	names'	נמס
instant (f.)	nemesa'	נמסה
instant coffee	nes kafe'	נס קפה
instead of	bimkom'	במקום
instructions	takhtiv'	תכתיב
insulation	bidud'	בידוד
insulator	mevoded'	מבודד
insurance	bitu'akh	ביטוח
intelligent (m.)	khakham'	חכם

intelligent (f.)	khakhama'	חכמה
intensity	otsma'	עוצמה
intercity	beynironi'	בינעירוני
interest	in"yan'	ענין
interesting	mean"yen'	מענין
interior	pnim	פנים
intermission	hafsaka'	הפסקה
internal (m.)	pnimi'	פנימי
internal (f.)	pnimit'	פנימית
interval	mirvakh' zman	מרווח זמן
interview	raayon'	ראיון
into	letokh'	לתוך
introduction	mavo'	מבוא
invest	lehashki'a	להשקיע
investigation	khakira'	חקירה
investment	hashkaa'	השקעה
invited (m.)	muzman'	מוזמן
invited (f.)	muzme'net	מוזמנת
iron (n.)	barzel'	ברזל
irregular	kharig'	חריג
irresponsibility	kho'ser akhrayut'	חוסר אחראיות
irrigation	hashkaya'	השקיה
is	yesh	יש
is cut	khatukh'	חתוך
is found	nimtsa'	נמצאה
is pessimistic	roe' shkhorot'	רואה שחורות
is sold	nimkar'	נמכר
is supposed to be	amur' lih"yot'	אמור להיות
is supposed to do	amur' laasot'	אמור לעשות
is (was) agreed	muskam'	מוסכם
is written	katuv'	כתוב
isn't it true?	haeyn' ze nakhon'?	האין זה נכון?
island	i	אי
Israel Museum	muzeon' israel'	מוזיאון ישראל
it	ze	זה
it can't be	lo yakhol' lih"yot'	לא יכול להיות
it costs	ze ole'	זה עולה
it could be	yakhol' lih"yot'	יכול להיות
it depends	ze talu'y	זה תלוי
it is...	ze...	זה...
it is forbidden	asur'!	אסור!
it is not possible	lo yitakhen'	לא יתכן
it is over	tam venishlam'	תם ונשלם
it sounds good	nishma' tov	נשמע טוב
it was	haya'	היה
it (was) learned	nilmad'	נלמד
it'll be o.k.	yihye' tov	יהיה טוב
it'll be o.k.	yihye' bese'der	יהיה בסדר
it's a fact	uvda'	עובדה
it's expensive	ze yakar'	זה יקר

it's senseless	eyn ta'am	אין טעם
it's too late	kvar meukhar'	כבר מאוחר
it's true that	nakhon' she...	נכון ש...
it's worthwhile	keday'	כדאי

J

jacket	jaket'	ז'קט
Jaffa Gate	sha'ar ya'fo	שער יפו
jam (n.)	riba'	ריבה
January	ya'nuar	ינואר
jeans	jins	ג'ינס
Jerusalem	yerushala'im	ירושלים
job	avoda'	עבודה
join	lehitstaref'	להצטרף
joint	meshutaf'	משותף
joke (n.)	bdikha'	בדיחה
Jordan	yarden'	ירדן
journal	ktav et'	כתב עת
journey	nesia'	נסיעה
judge (n.)	shofet'	שופט
judicial proceedings	halikhim' mishpatiim'	הליכים משפטיים
juice	mits	מיץ
July	yu'li	יולי
jump (n.)	kfitsa'	קפיצה
jumping	kfitsot'	קפיצות
June	yu'ni	יוני
just	stam	סתם
just (only)	rak	רק
just a bit	tip tipa'	טיפ־טיפה
just opened his mouth	rak patakh' et hape'	רק פתח את הפה
justice	tse'dek	צדק
justly	betse'dek	בצדק

K

keep (v.)	lishmor	לשמור
kept his promise	amad' behavtakhato'	עמד בהבטחתו
ketchup	ket'chup	קטצ'ופ
kettle	kumkum'	קומקום
key	mafte'yakh	מפתח
kick (v.)	liv"ot'	לבעוט
kilo	ki'lo	קילו
kind (adj.)	nadiv'	נדיב
kind (n.)	min, sug	מין; סוג
kind of	min	מין
kindergarten	gan yeladim'	גן ילדים

kiss (n.)	lenashek'	לנשק
kiss (v.)	neshika'	נשיקה
kitchen	mitbakh'	מטבח
knee	be'rekh	ברך
Knesset	kne'set	כנסת
Knesset members	khavrey' kne'set	חברי כנסת
knife (knives)	sakin' (sakinim')	סכין (סכינים)
know	lada'at	לדעת
knowledge	ye'da	ידע
kosher food	o'khel kasher'	אוכל כשר

L

laboratory	maabada'	מעבדה
ladder	sulam'	סולם
lady	gve'ret	גברת
lake	agam'	אגם
lamp	menora'	מנורה
land	kar'ka	קרקע
language	lashon'	לשון
lap	birka'im	ברכיים
large	gadol'	גדול
large number	hamon', mispar' gadol'	המון, מספר גדול
last (adj.)	akharon'	אחרון
last night	e'mesh	אמש
late	meukhar'	מאוחר
laugh (n.)	tskhok	צחוק
laundry	kvisa'	כביסה
law	khok	חוק
lawyer	o'rekh din	עורך דין
layer	shikhva'	שכבה
leader	manhig'	מנהיג
leap (v.)	likpots'	לקפוץ
learn	lilmod'	ללמוד
leather	or	עור
leave (v.)	laazov'	לעזוב
leave it alone!	azov' et ze!	עזוב את זה!
leave me alone!	taazov' oti'!	תעזוב אותי!
lecturer	martse'	מרצה
left	smol	שמאל
left side	tsad smol	צד שמאל
leg	re'gel	רגל
legend	agada'	אגדה
lemon	limon'	לימון
length	o'rekh	אורך
less	pakhot'	פחות
less than	pakhot' me...	פחות מ...
lesson	shiur'	שיעור
let	leharshot'	להרשות
let me	tarshe' li	תרשה לי

let him go	sheyelekh'	שילך
let him go to hell!	sheyelekh' leazazel'	שילך לעזאזל!
let me see	ten li lir"ot'	תן לי לראות
let's	ha'va	הבה
let's do it	bo naase'	בוא נעשה
let's hurry	keday' lehizdarez'	כדאי להזדרז
let's say that	nomar' she...	נאמר ש...
let's suppose	nani'yakh	נניח
letter	mikhtav'	מכתב
liar!	shakran'	שקרן!
library	sifriya'	ספריה
lie (v.)	lishkav'	לשכב
lie in the sun	lehishtazef'	להשתזף
life	khaim'	חיים
light (adj.), (m.)	kal	קל
light (adj.), (f.)	kala'	קלה
light (n.)	or	אור
light bulb	nura'	נורה
likable (m.)	khaviv'	חביב
likable (f.)	khaviva'	חביבה
like (v.)	leehov'	לאהוב
like (conj.)	kmo	כמו
like nothing	kmo klum	כמו כלום
like this (m.)	kaze'	כזה
like this (f.)	kazot'	כזאת
limit (n.)	gvul'	גבול
limit (v.)	lehagbil'	להגביל
limited	mugbal'	מוגבל
line	kav	קו
line *(in communication)*	kav ke'sher	קו קשר
lion	ariye'	אריה
lips	sfata'im	שפתיים
lipstick	o'dem	אודם
liquid	nozel'	נוזל
listen!	tishma'!	תשמע!
listen, you...	tishma' khabub'...	תשמע חבוב...
literature	sifrut'	ספרות
little	meat', ktsat	מעט, קצת
live (v.)	likh"yot'	לחיות
liver	kaved'	כבד
living room	salon'	סלון
load (n.)	o'mes	עומס
load (v.)	lehaamis'	להעמיס
loan (n.)	halvaa'	הלוואה
local time	shaon' mekomi'	שעון מקומי
lock (n.)	man"ul'	מנעול
lock (v.)	lin"ol'	לנעול
long	arokh'	ארוך
long ago	ze mikvar'	זה מכבר
look (n.)	mabat'	מבט

look (v.)	lir"ot'	לראות
look!	tir"e'!	תראה!
look for	lekhapes'	לחפש
looking back on it	bediavad'	בדיעבד
loose	rofef'	רופף
lost (m.)	avud'	אבוד
lost (f.)	avuda'	אבודה
lot	harbe'	הרבה
loud	kolani'	קולני
lousy feeling	hargasha' mezupe'tet	הרגשה מזופטת
love (v.)	leehov'	לאהוב
love (n.)	ahava'	אהבה
lover (m.)	meahev'	מאהב
lover (f.)	meahe'vet	מאהבת
low	namukh'	נמוך
lower	namukh' yoter'	נמוך יותר
lowest	hatakhton'	התחתון
luck	mazal'	מזל
lucky person	bar mazal'	בר מזל
luggage	mit"an'	מטען
lunch	arukhat' tsohora'im	ארוחת צהריים
lying down	mishkav'	משכב

M

machine	mekhona'	מכונה
mad	meshuga'	משוגע
magazine *(weekly)*	shvuon'	שבועון
Magen David *(emergency medical unit)*	magen' david'	מגן דוד
magic (n.)	kishuf'	כישוף
magnet	magnet'	מגנט
magnification	hagdala'	הגדלה
magnitude	go'del	גודל
maid	oze'ret	עוזרת
main	ikari'	עיקרי
main course	mana' ikarit'	מנה עיקרית
main thing	haikar'	העיקר
mainly, especially	beikar'	בעיקר
major (adj.)	rashi'	ראשי
majority	rov	רוב
make	laasot'	לעשות
make clear	lehav"hir'	להבהיר
male	zakhar'	זכר
mall	kan"yon'	קניון
malt beer	bi'ra shkhora'	בירה שחורה
manage (v.)	lehiistader'	להסתדר
manager	menahel'	מנהל
many	harbe'	הרבה
map	mapa'	מפה

map of the city	mapa' shel ha'ir	מפה של העיר
March	merts	מרץ
market	shuk	שוק
married	nasu'y	נשוי
marry	lehitkhaten'	להתחתן
marvelous	nifla'	נפלא
mashbir	mashbir'	משביר
mask (n.)	masekha'	מסכה
mass	ma'sa	מסה
masses	a'mkha	עמך
material	khomer'	חומר
math	kheshbon'	חשבון
mathematician	matematika'i	מתמטיקאי
matter	in"yan'	ענין
mattress	mizron'	מזרון
May	may	מאי
may	yakhol'	יכול
may I?	mutar' li	מותר לי?
may rise	asuy' laalot'	עשוי לעלות
me	oti'	אותי
mean (n.)	memutsa'	ממוצע
mean (v.)	lehitkaven'	להתכוון
mean (adj.)	beynoni'	ביניני
meanwhile	beynta'im	בינתיים
measurement	mdida'	מדידה
meat	basar'	בשר
meat (kashrut)	basari'	בשרי
mechanic	mekhonai'	מכונאי
medical center (sick fund)	kupat' kholim'	קופת חולים
medicine	refua'	רפואה
meet	lehipagesh'	להפגש
meet with	lehipagesh' im	להפגש עם
meeting	pgisha'	פגישה
melon	melon'	מלון
member	khaver'	חבר
memory	zikaron'	זכרון
men	anashim'	אנשים
menu	tafrit'	תפריט
mess	balagan'	בלגן
message	hodaa'	הודעה
metalworker	masger'	מסגר
method	shita'	שיטה
mice	akhbarim'	עכברים
microscope	mikroskop'	מיקרוסקופ
midday	tsohoray'im	צהרים
middle	em'tsa	אמצע
midnight	khatsot'	חצות
milk	khalav'	חלב
milk products	divrey' khalav'	דברי חלב

million	milion′	מיליון
mind (n.)	mo'akh	מוח
mindlessly	bli rosh	בלי ראש
mine (pron.)	sheli′	שלי
minimum	mi'nimum	מינימום
minister	sar	שר
Ministry	misrad′	משרד
Ministry of the Interior	misrad′ hapnim′	משרד הפנים
Ministry of Tourism	misrad′ hatayarut′	משרד התיירות
minority	miut′	מיעוט
minute (n.)	daka′	דקה
mirror	mar"a′	מראה
miscarriage	hapala′	הפלה
mistake (n.)	taut′, fash'la	טעות, פשלה
mix up	bilbul′	בלבול
mockingly	bela'ag	בלעג
modern	moder'ni	מודרני
modest (m.)	tsanu'a	צנוע
modest (f.)	tsnua′	צנועה
Monday	yom sheni′	יום שני
money	ke'sef	כסף
monotonous	khadgoni′	חדגוני
month	kho'desh	חודש
mood, bad mood	matsav′ ru'akh	מצב רוח
more	yoter′	יותר
more, still	od	עוד
more than	yoter′ measher′	יותר מאשר
more than anything	yoter′ mikol′	יותר מכל
more than this	yoter′ mize′	יותר מזה
moreover	ye'ter al ken	יתר על כן
morning	bo'ker	בוקר
mosque	misgad′	מסגד
mosquito (mosquitoes)	yetush′ (yetushim′)	יתוש (יתושים)
most	rov, hakhi′	רוב, הכי
most of the time	rov hazman′	רוב הזמן
most people	rov haanashim′	רוב האנשים
most probably	karov′ levaday′	קרוב לוודאי
mother	i'ma	אמא
motion	tnua′	תנועה
motor	mano'a	מנוע
mound	tel	תל
mountain	har	הר
mouse, mice	akhbar′, akhbarim′	עכבר, עכברים
mouth	pe	פה
move	lazuz′	לזוז
move aside!	zuz hatsi'da!	זוז הצידה!
movement	tnua′	תנועה

movie	se'ret	סרט
much	harbe'	הרבה
mug (n.)	se'fel	ספל
murder (n.)	re'tsakh	רצח
museum	muzeon'	מוזיאון
music	muz'ika	מוסיקה
my, mine	sheli'	שלי
my brother	akhi'	אחי
my children	hayeladim' sheli'	הילדים שלי
my friends	hayedidim'	הידידים
my group	hakvutsa' sheli'	הקבוצה שלי
my husband	baali'	בעלי
my luggage	hamizvadot' sheli'	המזוודות שלי
my name is	shmi'	שמי
my relatives	krovim' sheli'	קרובים שלי
my sister	akhoti'	אחותי

N

nail (nails)	masmer' (masmerim')	מסמר (מסמרים)
nails, fingernails	tsiporna'im	ציפורניים
name (n.)	shem	שם
narrow (m.)	tsar	צר
narrow (f.)	tsara'	צרה
nationality	leom'	לאום
natural (m.)	tiv"i'	טבעי
natural (f.)	tiv"it'	טבעית
nature	te'va	טבע
naughty (m.)	shovav'	שובב
naughty (f.)	shoveva'	שובבה
near	karov', leyad'	קרוב, ליד
near the sea	leyad' hayam'	ליד הים
near work	leyad' haavoda'	ליד העבודה
necessary	khayav'	חייב
necessary condition	tna'y bal yaavor'	תנאי בל יעבור
neck	tsavar'	צואר
need (v.)	tsarikh'	צריך
need (n.)	tso'rekh	צורך
need (have)	tsarikh'	צריך
needle	ma'khat	מחט
needs (has) to be	tsarikh' lih"yot'	צריך להיות
needs (has) to do	tsarikh' laasot'	צריך לעשות
neighbor	shakhen'	שכן
neighborhood	shkhuna'	שכונה
nervy (m.)	khutspan'	חוצפן
nervy (f.)	khutspanit'	חוצפנית
neutral	neitra'li	נייטרלי
never	af paam', af pa'am lo	אף פעם, אף פעם לא

never mind	eyn davar', lo khashuv', mey'le	אין דבר, לא חשוב, מילא
nevertheless	bekhol' zot	בכל זאת
new (m.)	khadash'	חדש
new (f.)	khadasha'	חדשה
news	khadashot'	חדשות
newspaper	iton'	עיתון
newspaper article	maamar' beiton'	מאמר בעיתון
next	haba'	הבא
next month	bekho'desh haba'	בחודש הבא
next to	leyad', karov' el	ליד, קרוב אל
next week	beshavu'a haba'	בשבוע הבא
next year	beshana' habaa'	בשנה הבאה
nice	yafe', nekhmad'	יפה, נחמד
nice vacation	khufsha' neima'	חופשה נעימה
night	lay'la	לילה
nightclub	moadon' la'yla	מועדון לילה
nine	tish"a'	תשעה
nine hundred	tsha meot'	תשע מאות
nineteen	tsha' esre'	תשע עשרה
ninety	tish"im'	תשעים
ninth	tshii'	תשיעי
no, not	lo	לא
no entry	eyn knisa'	אין כניסה
no exit	eyn yetsiya'	אין יציאה
no luck	eyn mazal'	אין מזל
no matter	eyn davar'	אין דבר
no one	af ekhad'	אף אחד
no one wants	af ekhad' lo rotse'	אף אחד לא רוצה
no problem	eyn shum baaya'	אין שום בעיה
no smoking	haishun' asur'	העישון אסור
no way!	lo ba bekheshbon'	לא בא בחשבון
nobody cares	lo' ikhpat' leaf ekhad'	לא איכפת לאף אחד
noise	ra'ash'	רעש
non-religious (m.)	khiloni'	חילוני
non-religious (f.)	khilonit'	חילונית
nonstop	lelo' hefsek'	ללא הפסק
nonsense!	shtuyot'!	שטויות!
nonsense, lies	bablat'	בבל"ט
noon	tsohora'im	צהריים
normal	norma'li	נורמלי
north	tsafon'	צפון
nose	af	אף
not	bilti', lo	בלתי, לא
not a lot	lo harbe'	לא הרבה
not at all	bikhlal' lo	בכלל לא
not certain	lo batu'akh	לא בטוח
not connected, related	lo kashur'	לא קשור
not everything	lo hakol'	לא הכל

not exactly	lo bediyuk'	לא בדיוק
not good	lo tov	לא טוב
not having a choice	beleyt' brera'	בלית ברירה
not in order to	lo bikhdey'	לא בכדי
not long ago	lo mizman'	לא מזמן
not pleasant	lo naim'	לא נעים
not possible	bil'ti efshari'	בלתי אפשרי
not really! **not necessarily**	lav dav'ka!	לאו דווקא!
not significant	lo mashmauti'	לא משמעותי
not so good	lo kol kakh'	לא כל כך
not so much	lo kol kakh harbe'	לא כל כך הרבה
not that!	lo ze!	לא זה!
not the same thing	lo oto' davar'	לא אותו דבר
not there	lo sham	לא שם
not this way	lo ka'kha	לא ככה
not useful	lo shimushi'	לא שמושי
not worthwhile	lo keday'	לא כדאי
not yet	od lo	עוד לא
notebook	makhbe'ret	מחברת
nothing	klum, meu'ma, shum davar'	כלום, מאומה, שום דבר
nothing new	shum davar' khadash'	שום דבר חדש
nothing remains	lo nish"ar' klum	לא נשאר כלום
nothing to do	eyn ma laasot'	אין מה לעשות
November	nove'mber	נובמבר
now	akhshav'	עכשיו
nucleus	gar"in'	גרעין
nudnik, pest	nud'nik	נודניק
number	mispar'	מיספר
number of	ka'ma	כמה
nurse (<u>n</u>.)	akhot'	אחות
nursery	pauton'	פעוטון
nut *(tool)*	um	אום
nut (nuts) *(food)*	egoz' (egozim')	אגוז (אגוזים)
nutrition	tzuna'	תזונה

O

oasis	nave' midbar'	נווה מדבר
object (aim)	matara'	מטרה
occasion	iru'a	אירוע
occupation *(work)*	isuk'	עיסוק
occupation *(land)*	kibush'	כיבוש
October	okto'ber	אוקטובר
of course	kamuvan', vaday', bevaday'	כמובן, ודאי, בודאי
of (somebody's)	shel	של
office	misrad'	משרד
officer	katsin'	קצין

often	leitim' krovot'	לעיתים קרובות
Oh my God!	oy vaavoy' li	אוי ואבוי לי
oil	she'men	שמן
o.k.	bese'der	בסדר
old (m.)	yashan'	ישן
old (f.)	yeshana'	ישנה
old (age) (m.)	zaken'	זקן
old (age) (f.)	zkena'	זקנה
Old City	hair haatika'	העיר העתיקה
olive, olives	za'it, zeytim'	זית, זיתים
olive trees	atsey' za'it	עצי זית
on	al, be..., le...	על, ב..., ל...
on a bus	beo'tobus	באוטובוס
on a trip	latiyul'	לטיול
on condition	al tna'y	על תנאי
on (day)	bayom'	ביום
on Friday evening	bee'rev shabat'	בערב שבת
on (from) the side	betsad'	בצד
on line	bator'	בתור
on probation	al tna'y	על תנאי
on purpose, purposely	bekhavana'	בכוונה
on Saturday evening	bemotsey' shabat'	במוצאי שבת
on suspicion of	bekhashad' shel	בחשד של
on the basis of	al smakh'	על סמך
on the beach	al sfat hayam'	על שפת הים
on the chair	al hakise'	על הכיסא
on the contrary	ad'raba	אדרבא
on the corner	bapina'	בפינה
on the first floor	bekoma' rishona'	בקומה ראשונה
on the floor	al haritspa'	על הרצפה
on the ground	al haadama'	על האדמה
on the red light *(traffic)*	beor' adom'	באור אדום
on the second floor	bekoma' shniya'	בקומה שניה
on the shore	bakhof'	בחוף
on the side	betsad'	בצד
on the table	al hashulkhan'	על השולחן
on the television	al hatelevi'ziya	על הטלוויזיה
on the top floor	bekoma' hael"yona'	בקומה העליונה
on time	bazman', bamoed'	בזמן, במועד
on what basis?	al smakh ma?	על סמך מה?
once	pa'am	פעם
one	ekhad', akhat'	אחד, אחת
one by one	ekhad' ekhad'	אחד אחד
one hundred	me'a	מאה
one of them	ekhad' mihem'	אחד מהם
one way or another	eykh' shehu'	איכשהו
onion	batsal'	בצל

only	rak, stam	רק, סתם
open (m.) (not closed)	patu'akh	פתוח
open (f.)	ptukha'	פתוחה
open (m.) *(not covered)*	galuy'	גלוי
open (f.)	gluya'	גלויה
open (v.)	lifto'akh	לפתוח
open the door	tiftakh' et hade'let	תפתח את הדלת
opened his mouth	patakh' et hape'	פתח את הפה
opener	potkhan'	פותחן
opening	ptikha'	פתיחה
openly	begalu'y	בגלוי
opposite	mul	מול
opposition	mitnagdim'	מתנגדים
or	o	או
orange (m.)	katom'	כתום
orange (f.)	ktuma'	כתומה
oranges	tapuzim'	תפוזים
order *(command)*	tsav	צו
order (n.)	se'der	סדר
order *(commission)*	hazmana'	הזמנה
order tickets	lehazmin' kartisim'	להזמין כרטיסים
orderly (m.)	mesudar'	מסודר
orderly (f.)	mesude'ret	מסודרת
ordinary	ragil'	רגיל
other	akher'	אחר
other than this	prat le ze	פרט לזה
otherwise	akhe'ret	אחרת
our, ours	shela'nu	שלנו
outside	bakhuts'	בחוץ
oven	tanur' afiya'	תנור אפיה

P

page	amud'	עמוד
paid parking	khanaya' betashlum'	חניה בתשלום
pain (n.)	keev'	כאב
painting	tsvia'	צביעה
pan (pans)	tavnit' (tavniyot')	תבנית (תבניות)
pants	mikhnasa'im	מכנסיים
paper	n"yar'	נייר
paper *(article)*	maamar' madai'	מאמר מדעי
papers *(documents)*	teudot'	תעודות
parallel	makbil'	מקביל
parallel to	bemakbil'	במקביל
pardon me!	slikha'	סליחה
parentheses	sogra'im	סוגריים
park	gan	גן
park (v.)	lakhnot'	לחנות
parking	khanaya'	חניה

parking lights	orot' khanaya'	אורות חניה
particular part	tsad mesuyam'	צד מסוים
particularly	bim"yukhad'	במיוחד
partner	shutaf'	שותף
pass (v.)	laavor'	לעבור
passed the test	amad' bamivkhan'	עמד במבחן
passenger	nose'a	נוסע
passport	darkon'	דרכון
passport control	biko'ret darkonim'	ביקורת דרכונים
passport number	mispar' darkon'	מספר דרכון
past	avar'	עבר
path	maslul'	מסלול
pattern	tavnit'	תבנית
patties	ktsitsot'	קציצות
pause (n.)	pe'sek zman	פסק זמן
pay (v.)	leshalem'	לשלם
pay at the register	shalem' bakupa'	שלם בקופה
payment	tashlum'	תשלום
PC	makhshev' ishi'	מחשב אישי
peace	shalom'	שלום
peace agreement	khoze' shalom'	חוזה שלום
peach	afarsek'	אפרסק
pear	agas'	אגס
pedal (n.)	davsha'	דוושה
pen	et	עט
pencil	iparon'	עיפרון
people	anashim'	אנשים
pepper	pilpel'	פלפל
perfect	metsuyan'	מצוין
perfectly all right, fine	bese'der gamur'	בסדר גמור
performance	bitsu'a	ביצוע
perfume	bo'sem	בושם
perhaps	ulay'	אולי
period *(time)*	makhzor'	מחזור
periodical	makhzori'	מחזורי
permanent	kavu'a	קבוע
permeable	khadir'	חדיר
perpendicular	meunakh'	מאונך
person	ish	איש
personal	ishi'	אישי
personnel	koach' adam'	כוח אדם
petrol	de'lek	דלק
phone (v.)	letalfen', letsaltsel'	לטלפן, לצלצל
photo (n.)	tatslum'	תצלום
photocopy (v.)	leshakhpel'	לשכפל
photograph (v.)	letsalem'	לצלם
physicist	fisika'i	פיסיקאי
physics	fi'sika	פיסיקה

piano	psanter'	פסנתר
pickled fish	dag malu'akh	דג מלוח
picture	tmuna'	תמונה
piece	khatikha'	חתיכה
pig!	khazir'!	חזיר!
pillow	karit'	כרית
pillowcase(s)	tsipa' (tsipot')	ציפה (ציפות)
pilot	tayas'	טיס
pin	sika'	סיכה
pineapple	ananas'	אננס
ping pong	te'nis shulkhan'	טניס שולחן
pink	varod'	ורוד
pipe	tsinor'	צינור
pity (n.)	khaval'	חבל
pity	khaval'	חבל
place	makom'	מקום
plain (adj.)	pashut'	פשוט
plan (n.)	tokhnit'	תוכנית
plan (v.)	letakhnen'	לתכנן
plane	matos'	מטוס
plank	ke'resh	קרש
plant *(garden)*	tse'makh	צמח
plant *(factory)*	mif''al'	מפעל
plantation	mata'	מטע
plaster (v.)	letayekh'	לטייח
plate	tsala'khat	צלחת
play (n.)	hatsaga', miskhak'	הצגה, משחק
play (v.)	lesakhek'	לשחק
playing cards	klafim'	קלפים
please	bevakasha', a'na	בבקשה, אנא
please (Arabic)	tfa'dal	תפדל
please listen	na lehakshiv'	נא להקשיב
please sit down	na lashe'vet	נא לשבת
pliers	pla'yer	פלייר
plug (n.)	she'ka	שקע
plum	shezif'	שזיף
pocket	kis	כיס
point (n.)	nekuda'	נקודה
poison	ra'al	רעל
pole	mot	מוט
police	mishtara'	משטרה
police department	mishtara'	משטרה
policeman (m.)	shoter'	שוטר
policeman (f.)	shote'ret	שוטרת
polite (m.)	adiv'	אדיב
polite (f.)	adiva'	אדיבה
pool	brekha'	בריכה
poor (m.)	ani'	עני
poor (f.)	aniya'	עניה
popular (m.)	mevukash'	מבוקש

popular (f.)	mevuke'shet	מבוקשת
population	okhlusiya'	אוכלוסיה
port	namal'	נמל
porter	sabal'	סבל
portion	mana'	מנה
position	emda'	עמדה
possibility	efsharut'	אפשרות
possible	efshar'	אפשר
Post	do'ar	דואר
post office	do'ar	דואר
postcard	gluya'	גלויה
pot	sir	סיר
potato	tapu'akh adama'	תפוח אדמה
potential	potentsial'	פוטנציאל
powder	avka'	אבקה
power	ko'akh	כח
practical (m.)	maasi'	מעשי
practical (f.)	maasit'	מעשית
pray	lehitpalel'	להתפלל
precious	yakar'	יקר
precise	meduyak'	מדויק
precisely	bimduyak'	במדויק
preface	mavo'	מבוא
prefer	lehaadif'	להעדיף
prepare	lehakhin'	להכין
present (n.)	matana'	מתנה
president	nasi'	נשיא
press (n.)	tiksho'ret	תקשורת
press (v.)	lilkhots'	ללחוץ
pressure	la'khats	לחץ
prevent	limno'a	למנוע
previous	hakodem'	הקודם
previously	lifney' khen	לפני כן
price (n.)	mkhir'	מחיר
primary	ikari'	עיקרי
Prime Minister	rosh hamimshala'	ראש הממשלה
principal	menahel'	מנהל
print (v.)	lehadpis'	להדפיס
printer	madpe'set	מדפסת
prison	beit ke'le	בית כלא
private	prati'	פרטי
problem	baaya'	בעיה
proceed	lehitkadem'	להתקדם
process (n.)	tahalikh'	תהליך
processed	meubad'	מעובד
processing	ibud'	עיבוד
producer	yatsran'	יצרן
production	yetsur'	ייצור
production manager	menahel' yetsur'	מנהל ייצור

profession	miktso'a	מקצוע
profit (n.)	re'vakh	רווח
program	tokhnit'	תכנית
progress (n.)	hitkadmut'	התקדמות
progressive	mitkadem'	מתקדם
promise	havtakha'	הבטחה
prophet	navi '	נביא
propose	lehatsi'a	להציע
prostitute	zona'	זונה
protect	lehagen'	להגן
protection	hagana'	הגנה
prove	lehokhi'yakh	להוכיח
provisions	mitsrakhim'	מצרכים
pub	pub	פאב
publicly	befumbey'	בפומבי
puncture	te'ker, pan'cher	תקר, פנצ׳ר
purchase (n.)	kniya'	קניה
purpose	matara', kavana'	מטרה, כוונה
purposely	bemitkaven'	במתכוון

Q

quality	eykhut'	איכות
quantity	kamut'	כמות
quarantine	hesger'	הסגר
quarter (¼)	re'va	רבע
question (n.)	sheela'	שאלה
question mark	siman' sheela'	סימן שאלה
questionnaire	sheelon'	שאלון
quick (m.)	zariz'	זריז
quick (f.)	zriza'	זריזה
quickly	maher'	מהר
quiet (adj.) (m.)	ragu'a	רגוע
quiet (adj.) (f.)	regua'	רגועה
quietly	beshe'ket	בשקט

R

rabbi	rav	רב
rabbit	shafan'	שפן
race (n.)	meruts'	מרוץ
radiation	krina'	קרינה
radiator	radia'tor	רדיאטור
radio	ra'dio	רדיו
rag	smartut'	סמרטוט
railway	rake'vet	רכבת
rain (n.)	ge'shem	גשם
rainy	gashum'	גשום
raise (v.)	leharim'	להרים
rapid	mahir'	מהיר

rare	nadir′	נדיר
rarely	leitim′ rekhokot′	לעיתים רחוקות
raspberry	pe′tel	פטל
raspberry drink	mits pe′tel	מיץ פטל
rate (n.)	taarif′	תעריף
rate of exchange	sha′ar khalifin′	שער חליפין
raw material	kho′mer ge′lem	חומר גלם
ray	ke′ren	קרן
razor blade	sakin′ gilu′akh	סכין גילוח
reach	lehasig′	להשיג
reaching a decision	kabalat′ hakhlata′	קבלת החלטה
read	likro′	לקרוא
read it!	kra′ et ze	קרא את זה
reading	kria′	קריאה
ready	mukhan′	מוכן
real	amiti′	אמיתי
realize	lehavin′	להבין
really	bekhayay′	בחיי
rear end	yashvan′	ישבן
reason (n.)	siba′	סיבה
reasonable	mani′akh et hada′at	מניח את הדעת
receipt	kabala′	קבלה
receive	lekabel′	לקבל
recently	lo mizman′	לא מזמן
reception	kabala′	קבלה
reception *(of someone)*	kabalat′ panim′	קבלת פנים
recognition	hakara′	הכרה
recommend	lehamlits′	להמליץ
recommended	mumlats′	מומלץ
record (n.)	taklit′	תקליט
record (v.)	lehaklit′	להקליט
recorder	muklat′	מוקלט
recover	lehavri′	להבריא
red (m.)	adom′	אדום
red (f.)	aduma′	אדומה
Red Sea	yam suf	ים סוף
red wine	ya′in adom′	יין אדום
reddish	adamdam′	אדמדם
reduce (v.)	lehaktin′, lehorid′	להקטין, להוריד
refer	lehityakhes′ el	להתיחס אל
reference	izkur′	אזכור
refine	lezakekh′	לזכך
reflection	hakhzara′	החזרה
refrigerator	mekarer′	מקרר
refund (v.)	lehakhzir	להחזיר
refuse (v.)	lesarev′	לסרב
regards	drishat′ shalom′	דרישת שלום
region	ezor′	איזור
regular	ragil′	רגיל

regular lights	orot′ namukhim′	אורות נמוכים
rehearsal	khazara′	חזרה
relation	ya′khas	יחס
relative	karov′ mishpakha′	קרוב משפחה
relatives	krovey′ mishpakha′	קרובי משפחה
religion	dat	דת
religious (m.)	dati′	דתי
religious (f.)	datiya′	דתיה
rent a room	liskor′ khe′der	לשכור חדר
rent-a-car companies	khevrot′ le haskarat′ re′khev	חברות להשכרת רכב
repeat (v.)	lakhzor′ al	לחזור על
representative	natsig′	נציג
request (n.)	bakasha′	בקשה
request (v.)	levakesh′	לבקש
research (n.)	mikhkar′	מחקר
researcher	khoker′	חוקר
residual	shiyuri′	שיורי
resistance	hitnagdut′	התנגדות
resolution	hakhlata′	החלטה
resolution *(phys.)*	ko′sher hafrada′	כושר הפרדה
resonance (n.)	tehuda′	תהודה
respiratory diseases	makhalot′ darkey′ neshima′	מחלות דרכי נשימה
responsibility	akhrayut′	אחריות
responsible	akhrai′	אחראי
rest (n.)	menukha′	מנוחה
rest (v.)	lanu′akh	לנוח
restaurant	mis″ada′	מסעדה
restrooms	shirutim′	שירותים
return (n.)	khazara′	חזרה
return (v.)	lehakhzir′	להחזיר
return home	lakhzor′ habay′ta	לחזור הביתה
reverse (adj.)	akho′ra	אחורה
review (n.)	maamar′ makif′	מאמר מקיף
rice	o′rez	אורז
rich (m.)	ashir′	עשיר
rich (f.)	ashira′	עשירה
ride (n.)	hasaa′	הסעה
right (rights)	zkhut′ (zkhuyot′)	זכות (זכויות)
right *(correct)*	nakhon′	נכון
right? true?	nakhon′?	נכון?
right *(opposite to left)*	yami′na	ימינה
right here	po bamakom′	פה במקום
right now	kvar akhshav′	כבר עכשיו
right side	tsad yamin′	צד ימין
ring (n.)	taba′at	טבעת
rise (v.)	laalot′	לעלות
risk (n.)	sakana′	סכנה
risky	mesukan′	מסוכן

river	nahar'	נהר
road	kvish	כביש
road accident	teunat' drakhim'	תאונת דרכים
road sign	tamrur'	תמרור
roast (n.)	tsli'	צלי
robe (n.)	khaluk'	חלוק
room (n.)	khe'der	חדר
room, place	makom'	מקום
root	sho'resh	שורש
rope (n.)	khe'vel	חבל
rope, string	khut	חוט
rose (v.)	ala'	עלה
rose (n.)	ve'red	ורד
rotation	rota'tsiya	רוטציה
rough (m.)	mekhuspas', gas	מחוספס, גס
rough (f.)	mekhuspe'set, gasa'	מחוספסת, גסה
route	de'rekh	דרך
rowdy (m.)	mitpare'a	מתפרע
rowdy (f.)	mitpara'at	מתפרעת
rubber	gu'mi	גומי
rug	shati'yakh	שטיח
rumor (rumors)	shmua' (shmuot')	שמועה (שמועות)
run (v.)	laruts'	לרוץ
run quickly!	ruts maher'!	רוץ מהר!
running	ritsa'	ריצה
rural settlement	moshav'	מושב
rust	khaluda'	חלודה

S

Sabbath	shabat'	שבת
sack (n.)	sak	שק
sad	atsuv'	עצוב
safe	batu'akh	בטוח
safety	betikhut'	בטיחות
salad	salat'	סלט
salami	naknik'	נקניק
salary	masko'ret	משכורת
sale (n.)	mkhira'	מכירה
sale item	mitsrakh'	מצרך
salesman	mokher'	מוכר
saleswoman	mokhe'ret	מוכרת
salon	mispara'	מספרה
salt	me'lakh	מלח
saltwater fish	dagey' yam	דגי ים
salty (m.)	malu'akh	מלוח
salty (f.)	mlukha'	מלוחה
same thing	oto' davar'	אותו דבר
sand	khol	חול

satisfactory	masbi’ah ratson’	משביע רצון
satisfied	merutse’	מרוצה
saturation	revaya’	רוויה
Saturday	shabat’	שבת
sauce	ro’tev	רוטב
save (v.)	lehatsil’	להציל
saw (n.)	masor’	משור
say (v.)	lehagid’, lomar’	להגיד, לומר
saying	amira’	אמירה
scale	mozna’im	מאזניים
scan (v.)	lisrok’	לסרוק
scanner	sorek’	סורק
scary	mafkhid’	מפחיד
scholar	melumad’	מלומד
school	beit se’fer	בית ספר
school book	se’fer limud’	ספר לימוד
science	mada’	מדע
scientist	mad“an’	מדען
scorpion	akrab’	עקרב
(scorpions)	(akrabim’)	(עקרבים)
screw (n.)	bo’reg	בורג
screwdriver	mavreg’	מברג
sculpture	pe’sel	פסל
sea	yam’	ים
search (v.)	lekhapes’	לחפש
search for	khipusim’ akharey’	חיפושים אחרי
seashore	hof, khof hayam’	חוף, חוף הים
season	una’	עונה
seat belt	khagura’t betihut’	חגורת בטיחות
seating	yeshiva’	ישיבה
second (n.)	shniya’	שנייה
second (adj.), (m.)	sheni’	שני
second (adj.), (f.)	shniya’	שניה
second portion	mana’ shniya’	מנה שניה
secret	sod	סוד
secretary (f.)	mazkira’	מזכירה
secretly	bekhashay’	בחשאי
security	bitakhon’	ביטחון
see (v.)	lir“ot’	לראות
see you!	lehitraot’!	להתראות!
seemingly	kivyakhol’	כביכול
seems	nir“e’	נראה
seldom	leitim’ rekhokot’	לעיתים רחוקות
selection	bkhira’	בחירה
self-service	shirut’ atsmi’	שירות עצמי
sell (v.)	limkor’	למכור
semiconductor	molikh’ lemakhatsa’	מוליך למחצה
send	lishlo’akh	לשלוח
sensitive (m.)	ragish’	רגיש
sensitive (f.)	regisha’	רגישה

separate (v.)	lehafrid′	להפריד
separately	benifrad′	בנפרד
September	septem′ber	ספטמבר
serious	retsini′	רציני
serious illness	makhala′ kasha′	מחלה קשה
serious mistake	fash′la retsinit′	פשלה רצינית
seriously	bekhol′ hartsinut′	בכל הרצינות
set (v.)	likbo′a	לקבוע
set (adj.)	kavu′a	קבוע
settled	meyushav′	מיושב
settlement	yeshuv′	ישוב
seven	shiv"a′	שבעה
seven thousand	shivat′ alafim′	שבעת אלפים
seventeen	shva′ esre′	שבע עשרה
seventh	shvii′	שביעי
seventy	shiv"im′	שבעים
several	akhadim′	אחדים
several times	peamim′ akhadot′, kama′ peamim′	פעמים אחדות, כמה פעמים
sewage	biyuv′	ביוב
sex	min	מין
sexual	mini′	מיני
Shabbat	shabat′	שבת
shade (n.)	gavan′	גוון
shake (v.)	lenaer′	לנער
shallow (m.)	radud′	רדוד
shallow (f.)	rduda′	רדודה
shampoo	shampo′	שמפו
shape (n.)	tsura′	צורה
share (v.)	leshatef′	לשתף
sharp	khad	חד
she	hi	היא
sheep	ke′ves	כבש
sheet (sheets)	sadin′ (sdinim′)	סדין (סדינים)
sheet metal	pakh	פח
shine (v.)	lehavrik′	להבריק
ship (n.)	sfina′	ספינה
shirt	khultsa′	חולצה
shoe	na′al	נעל
shoes	naala′im	נעליים
shoot (v.)	lirot′	לירות
shop (n.)	khanut′	חנות
shopping	kniyiot′	קניות
shore	khof′	חוף
short (m.)	katsar′, namukh′	קצר, נמוך
short (f.)	ktsara′, nemukha′	נמוכה, קצרה
shortly	biktsara′	בקצרה
shorts	shor′tim	שורטים
shot (n.)	yeriya′	יריה
shoulder	katef′	כתף

show (n.)	hatsaga'	הצגה
show (v.)	lehatsig'	להציג
shower	mikla'khat	מקלחת
shut up!	shtok	שתוק!
shut up already	shtok' kvar	שתוק כבר
sick (m.)	khole'	חולה
sick (f.)	khola'	חולה
sick fund	kupat' kholim'	קופת חולים
side (n.)	tsad	צד
side (v.)	letsoded'	לצודד
side by side	tsad betsad'	צד בצד
side dish	tose'fet	תוספת
sight	mar"e'	מראה
sightseeing	tiyul'	טיול
silence (n.)	she'ket	שקט
silent	shaket'	שקט
silently	beshe'ket	בשקט
silk	me'shi	משי
simple	pashut'	פשוט
since	meaz'	מאז
since when?	mimatay'?	ממתי?
sing	lashir'	לשיר
single	yakhid'	יחיד
sit	lashe'vet	לשבת
sit down! sit!	shev!	שב!
sit quietly	shev beshe'ket	שב בשקט!
site	atar'	אתר
situation	matsav'	מצב
six	shisha'	שישה
six days	shisha' yamim'	שישה ימים
sixteen	shesh esre'	שש עשרה
sixth	shishi'	שישי
sixty	shishim'	שישים
size (n.)	go'del	גודל
skeleton	she'led	שלד
skin	or	עור
skin disorders	makhalot' or	מחלות עור
skirt	khatsait'	חצאית
sky	raki'a	רקיע
slap, contradiction	stira'	סתירה
sleep (v.)	lishon'	לשון
sleep (n.)	shena'	שינה
sleeve	sharvul'	שרוול
slice of bread	prusat' le'khem	פרוסת לחם
slide (n.)	maglesha'	מגלשה
slight (adj.)	khalash'	חלש
slight bruise	srita' ktana'	סריטה קטנה
slight hesitation	tsel shel hisus'	צל של היסוס
slippers	naaley' ba'yt	נעלי בית
slow (m.)	iti'	איטי

slow (f.)	itit'	איטית
slowly	leat'	לאט
small (m.)	katan'	קטן
small (f.)	ktana'	קטנה
small cup	kosit', kosiyot'	כוסית, כוסיות
small number	mispar' katan'	מספר קטן
smoke (v.)	leashen'	לעשן
smoke (n.)	ashan'	עשן
smoked fish	dag meushan'	דג מעושן
smooth (m.)	khalak'	חלק
smooth (f.)	khalaka'	חלקה
smoothly	khad vekhalak'	חד וחלק
snake (snakes)	na'khash (nakhashim')	נחש (נחשים)
snob (m.)	mitnase'	מתנשא
snob (f.)	mitnaset'	מתנשאת
snow (n.)	she'leg	שלג
so	kakh, ka'kha, kol kakh'	כך, ככה, כל כך
so beautiful	kol kakh' yafe'	כל כך יפה
so how was it?	nu eykh haya'	נו, איך היה
so what?	az ma	אז מה?
so-so	ka'kha ka'kha	ככה ככה
soap	sabon'	סבון
soccer	kadure'gel	כדורגל
society	khevra'	חברה
socket	te'ka	תקע
socks	garba'im	גרביים
soft (m.)	rakh	רך
soft (f.)	raka'	רכה
soil	adama'	אדמה
solder	halkhama'	הלחמה
soldier (m.)	khayal'	חייל
soldier (f.)	khaye'let	חיילת
soldiers	khayalim'	חיילים
solution	pitaron'	פתרון
some kind of (m.)	ey'ze shehu'	איזה שהוא
some kind of (f.)	ey'zo shehi'	איזו שהיא
some sort of (m.)	ey'ze shehu'	איזה שהוא
some sort of (f.)	ey'zo shehi'	איזו שהיא
someone	mi'shehu	מישהו
something	ma'shehu	משהו
something else	ma'shehu akher'	משהו אחר
something strange	ma'shehu muzar'	משהו מוזר
something suitable	ma'shehu mat"im'	משהו מתאים
sometimes	lif'amim', leitim'	לפעמים, לעיתים
somewhere	ey'fo shehu'	איפה שהוא
son	ben	בן
son of a bitch	ben zona'	בן זונה
soon	bekarov'	בקרוב
sorry!	mitstaer'!	מצטער!
sort (n.)	sug	סוג

soup	marak'	מרק
sour (m.)	khamuts'	חמוץ
sour (f.)	khamutsa'	חמוצה
sour cream	shame'net	שמנת
south	darom'	דרום
souvenir	mazke'rot	מזכרת
speak	ledaber'	לדבר
speak up!	daber'!	דבר!
special	meyukhad'	מיוחד
special invitation	hazmana' meyukhe'det	הזמנה מיוחדת
speed (n.)	mhirut'	מהירות
spend	lehotsi' ke'sef	להוציא כסף
spend time	levalot'	לבלות
spicy (m.)	kharif'	חריף
spicy (f.)	kharifa'	חריפה
spoiled (m.)	mekulkal'	מקולקל
spoiled (f.)	mekulke'let	מקולקלת
sponge (n.)	sfog'	ספוג
spoon, spoons	kaf, kapot'	כף, כפות
spray (v.)	lehatiz'	להתיז
spray (n.)	tarkhif'	תרחיף
spring (n.)	kfitsa'	קפיץ
sprint (n.)	ritsa' le me'a me'ter	ריצה ל־100 מטר
square *(shape)*	ribu'a	ריבוע
squash (n.)	kishuim'	קישואים
stable (n.)	re'fet	רפת
stable (adj.)	yatsiv'	יציב
stability	yatsivut'	יציבות
stairs	madregot'	מדרגות
stand (n.)	emda'	עמדה
stand (v.)	laamod'	לעמוד
stand up	lakum'	לקום
standing up	beamida'	בעמידה
star	kokhav'	כוכב
start (v.)	lehatkhil'	להתחיל
start (n.)	hatkhala'	התחלה
state (n.)	mdina'	מדינה
station	takhana'	תחנה
stay	lehishaer'	להשאר
steak	stek'	סטיק
steel	plada'	פלדה
steering wheel	he'ge	הגה
stewardess	daye'let	דיילת
stick (n.)	makel'	מקל
still	od	עוד
stingy (m.)	kamtsan'	קמצן
stingy (f.)	kamtsanit'	קמצנית
stock (n.)	mlay	מלאי
stomach	be'ten	בטן
stop (v.)	laazor'	לעצור

stop!	atsor'!	עצור!
stop it!	tafsik'!	תפסיק!
stop sign	tamrur' atsor'	תמרור עצור
store (n.)	khanut'	חנות
storeroom	makhsan'	מחסן
story	sipur'	סיפור
straight	yashar'	ישר
strange	muzar'	מוזר
strange reaction	tguva' muzara'	תגובה מוזרה
street	rkhov'	רחוב
strength	kho'zek	חוזק
stress (n.)	maamats'	מאמץ
strong	khazak'	חזק
strong wind	ru'akh khazaka'	רוח חזקה
stubborn (m.)	akshan'	עקשן
stubborn (f.)	akshanit'	עקשנית
student (m.)	student'	סטודנט
student (f.)	studen'tit	סטודנטית
study (v.)	lilmod'	ללמוד
studying	limud'	לימוד
stuffy, suffocating	makhnik'	מחניק
submarine	tsole'let	צוללת
succeed in	lehatsli'yakh be...	להצליח ב...
success	hatslakha'	הצלחה
suddenly	pit"om'	פתאום
suffer (v.)	lisbol'	לסבול
sugar	sukar'	סוכר
suicide	hit"abdut'	התאבדות
suitable	rau'i	ראוי
suitable work	avoda' mat"ima'	עבודה מתאימה
suitcase	mizvada', mizvadot'	מזוודה, מזוודות
sum	skhum	סכום
summary	sikum'	סיכום
summer	ka'yts	קיץ
sun	she'mesh	שמש
Sunday	yom rishon'	יום ראשון
sunflower seeds	gar"inim'	גרעינים
sunrise	zrikhat' she'mesh	זריחת שמש
suntan lotion	krem shizuf'	קרם שיזוף
supermarket	supermar'ket	סופרמרקט
supply (n.)	aspaka'	אספקה
support (n.)	tmikha'	תמיכה
supporters	tomkhim'	תומכים
suppose	lehani'yakh	להניח
sure (adj.)	batu'akh	בטוח
sure!	bekhayay'! be'takh!	בחיי! בטח!
surface (n.)	pney she'takh	פני שטח
surgery	kirurgi'ya	כירורגיה
surprised	mufta'	מופתע

survive	lisrod'	לשרוד
suspect (v.)	lakhshod'	לחשוד
suspense movie	se'ret me'takh	סרט מתח
sweater	sve'der	סוודר
sweet (m.)	matok'	מתוק
sweet (f.)	metuka'	מתוקה
sweet dreams	khalomot' metukim'	חלומות מתוקים
sweetheart	mo'tek	מותק
swim in the sea	liskhot' bayam'	לשחות בים
swimming	skhiya'	שחיה
swimming pool	brekha'	בריכה
syllabus	tokhnit' limudim'	תוכנית לימודים
system	maare'khet	מערכת

T

table (tables)	shulkhan' (shulkhanot')	שולחן (שולחנות)
tablecloth	mapa'	מפה
tablespoon	kaf	כף
take	laka'khat	לקחת
take care of yourself	lishmor' al atsmekha'	לשמור על עצמך
tall (m.)	gavo'a	גבוה
tall (f.)	gvoha'	גבוהה
tangerines, oranges	klemanti'not	קלמנטינות
tank, container	meykhal'	מיכל
tape (n.)	nyar' de'vek	נייר דבק
target (n.)	matara'	מטרה
taste (n.)	ta'am	טעם
taste (v.)	lit"om'	טעם
tasty (m.)	taim'	טעים
tasty (f.)	teima'	טעימה
tax (n.)	mas	מס
taxi (service)	moniyot' (sherut')	מוניות (שרות)
tea	te	תה
teach	lelamed'	ללמד
teacher	more'	מורה
teaspoon	kapit' (kapiyot')	כפית (כפיות)
technician	tekhnai'	טכנאי
teeth	shina'im	שיניים
telephone	te'lefon	טלפון
television	televi'zia	טלוויזיה
tell	lehagid', lomar'	להגיד, לומר
tell me	tagid' li	תגיד לי
tell me, please	tagid' bevakasha'	תגיד בבקשה
temperature	khom, temperatu'ra	חום, טמפרטורה
temporary	zmani'	זמני
ten (f.)	e'ser	עשר
ten (m.)	asara'	עשרה
ten thousand	ase'ret alafim'	עשרת אלפים

tennis	te'nis	טניס
tensely	bidrikhut'	בדריכות
tension	metakh'	מתח
tent	o'hel	אוהל
tenth	asiri'	עשירי
tepid water	ma'im poshrim'	מים פושרים
test	mivkhan'	מבחן
thank God	barukh' hashem'	ברוך השם
thank (v.)	lehodot'	להודות
thank you	toda'	תודה
thanks a lot	toda' raba'	תודה רבה
that	asher', she...	אשר, ש...
that is because...	ze biglal' she...	זה בגלל ש...
that is to say	zot ome'ret	זאת אומרת
that it isn't so	ze' lo nakhon'	זה לא נכון
that means	zot ome'ret	זאת אומרת
that's boring	ze meshaamem'	זה משעמם
that's enough	ze maspik'	זה מספיק
that's final	nekuda'!	נקודה!
that's foolish	ze tipshi'	זה טפשי
that's good	ze tov	זה טוב
that's it	ze'hu ze	זהו זה
that's nice	ze yafe'	זה יפה
that's not enough	ze lo maspik'	זה לא מספיק
the Church of the Holy Sepulchre	knesiyat' hake'ver	כנסיית הקבר
the point is	hanekuda' hi	הנקודה היא
the result of	po'al yotse' min...	פועל יוצא מן...
the Temple Mount	har habait'	הר הבית
the type that	kaze' she...	כזה ש...
the Western Wall	hako'tel	הכותל
theater	teatron'	תאטרון
theft	gniva'	גניבה
then	az	אז
there	sham	שם
there is/are	yesh	יש
there is a need	yesh tso'rekh	יש צורך
there is/are not	eyn	אין
there isn't	eyn	אין
there is no choice	eyn brera'	אין ברירה
there is no doubt	eyn shum safek'	אין שום ספק
there is no need	eyn tso'rekh	אין צורך
there is no reason	eyn shum siba'	אין שום סיבה
there is no way	eyn shum efsharut'	אין שום אפשרות
there was a(n.) (m.)	haya'	היה
there was a(n.) (m.)	hayta'	היתה
there will be (m.)	yihye'	יהיה
there will be (f.)	tih"ye'	תהיה
therefore	i-lekhakh	אי לכך
thermometer	mad' khom	מד חום

these	ey'le, ey'lu	אילה, אילו
these memories	hazikhronot' hae'le	הזכרונות האלה
these things	hadvarim' haey'lu	הדברים האלו
they (m.)	hem	הם
they (f.)	hen	הן
thick (m.)	ave'	עבה
thick (f.)	ava'	עבה
thief	ganav'	גנב
thin (m.)	dak	דק
thin (f.)	daka	דקה
thing	davar'	דבר
think	lakhshov'	לחשוב
thinks ahead	khoshev' merosh'	חושב מראש
third	shlishi'	שלישי
thirteen	shlosh' esre'	שלוש עשרה
thirty	shloshim'	שלושים
thirty-one	shloshim' veakhat'	שלושים ואחת
this (m.)	ze	זה
this (f.)	zot, zo	זאת, זו
this form	hato'fes haze'	הטופס הזה
this is a, an	ze	זה
this is for	ze bishvil'	זה בשביל
this man	haish' haze'	האיש הזה
this place	hamakom' haze'	המקום הזה
this thing	hadavar' haze'	הדבר הזה
this way	kakh	כך
thought (n.)	makhshava'	מחשבה
thousand	e'lef	אלף
thousandth	alpit'	אלפית
three (m.)	shlosha'	שלושה
three (f.)	shalosh'	שלוש
three days	shlosha yamim'	שלושה ימים
three hundred	shlosh meot'	שלוש מאות
three thousand	shlo'shet alafim'	שלושת אלפים
three weeks	shlosha' shvuot'	שלושה שבועות
throat	garon'	גרון
through	be'ad	בעד
thumb	agudal'	אגודל
Thursday	yom khamishi'	יום חמישי
thus	kakh, ka'kha, lekhekh'	כך, ככה, לכך
ticket	kartis'	כרטיס
till	ad	עד
till the end	ad hasof'	עד הסוף
time	zman	זמן
time after time	pa'am akhar' pa'am	פעם אחר פעם
tin	pakh	פח
tip	te'sher	תשר
tire (tires)	tsamig' (tsmigim')	צמיג (צמיגים)
tired (m.)	ayef'	עייף
tired (f.)	ayefa'	עייפה

to	el, le...	אל, ל...
to a doctor	lerofe'	לרופא
to all this	el kol ze	אל כל זה
to become (an)	lehafokh' le...	להפוך ל...
to me	li	לי
to the left	smo'la	שמאלה
to the right	yami'na	ימינה
to town	hai'ra, lair'	העירה, לעיר
to where?	lean'?	לאן?
toast (n.)	tost	טוסט
today	hayom'	היום
together	ya'khad	יחד
toilet	shirutim'	שירותים
toilet paper	nyar' tualet'	נייר טואלט
tomato	agvaniyot'	עגבניות
tomorrow	makhar'	מחר
tongue	lashon'	לשון
too	miday'	מדי
too, also	gam	גם
too little	meat' miday'	מעט מדי
too much	yoter' miday'	יותר מדי
tool (tools)	kli (kelim')	כלי (כלים)
tooth	shen	שן
toothbrush	mivre'shet shina'im	מברשת שיניים
top	khe'lek el"yon'	חלק עליון
total	kolel'	כולל
total darkness	kho'shekh mitsra'im	חושך מצריים
touch (n.)	maga'	מגע
tourist	tayar'	תייר
towards	likrat'	לקראת
towel	mage'vet	מגבת
town	ir	עיר
toy	tsaatsu'a	צעצוע
tractor	tra'ktor	טרקטור
trade (n.)	miskhar'	מסחר
trade union	igud' miktsoi'	איגוד מקצועי
traffic	tnua'	תנועה
traffic police	mishte'ret tnua'	משטרת תנועה
train (n.)	rake'vet	רכבת
training	hit"amlut'	התעמלות
transparent	shakuf'	שקוף
transport (n.)	takhbura'	תחבורה
transportation	hasaa'	הסעה
travel (v.)	linso'a	לנסוע
travel (n.)	nesiya'	נסיעה
travel agency	sokhnut' nesiyot'	סוכנות נסיעות
travel agent (f.)	sokhe'net nesiyot'	סוכנת נסיעות
tray	magash'	מגש
tree (trees)	ets (etsim')	עץ (עצים)
tremendous, great	atsum'	עצום

trip (n.)	tiyul'	טיול
trousers	mikhnasa'im	מכנסיים
truck	masait'	משאית
truth	emet'	אמת
try (v.)	lenasot'	לנסות
Tuesday	yom shlishi'	יום שלישי
turkey	ho'du	הודו
turn (v.)	lesovev'	לסובב
turn around	lehistovev'	להסתובב
TV	televi'ziya	טלוויזיה
twelve	shneim' asar'	שנים עשר
twenty	esrim'	עשרים
twice	paama'im	פעמיים
twins	teumim'	תאומים
two (m.)	shna'im	שניים
two (f.)	shta'im	שתיים

U

ultimately	besofo' shel davar'	בסופו של דבר
umbrella	metriya'	מטריה
unable	lo yakhol'	לא יכול
unanimous	pe ekhad'	פה אחד
uncle	dod	דוד
uncomfortable	lo no'akh	לא נוח
unconscious	lelo' hakara'	ללא הכרה
under	mita'khat	מתחת
undershirt	gufiya'	גופיה
understand	lehavin'	להבין
understandingly	bitvuna'	בתבונה
underwear	levanim'	לבנים
undoubtedly	barur' meal' lekhol' safek'	ברור מעל לכל ספק
unfortunate (m.)	umlal'	אומלל
unfortunate (f.)	umlala'	אומללה
unification	ikhud'	איחוד
uniform (adj.)	akhid'	אחיד
uniform (n.)	madim'	מדים
unintentionally	belo' khavana'	בלא כוונה
universal	olami', kolel'	עולמי, כולל
university	univer'sita	אוניברסיטה
unless	ilmale'	אלמלא
unloading	horadat' o'mes	הורדת עומס
unnecessary	meyutar'	מיותר
unpleasant	lo naim'	לא נעים
unsuitable	lo mat"im'	לא מתאים
until	ad	עד
until here	ad kan'	עד כאן
until now	ad ko'	עד כה
until the end	ad hasof'	עד הסוף

English	Transliteration	Hebrew
until then	ad az	עד אז
until when?	ad matay'?	עד מתי?
up	lema'ala	למעלה
up to	ad	עד
upper	el"yon'	עליון
upset	nis"ar'	נסער
urgent	dakhuf'	דחוף
urine	she'ten	שתן
us	ota'nu	אותנו
use	shimush'	שימוש
used to	ragil' le...	רגיל ל...
useful	moil'	מועיל
useless	lelo' hoil'	ללא הועיל
usual	mekubal'	מקובל
usually	bede'rekh klal	בדרך כלל

V

English	Transliteration	Hebrew
valid	beto'kef	בתוקף
value (values)	e'rekh (arakhim')	ערך (ערכים)
vegetables	yerakot'	ירקות
vehicle	re'khev	רכב
vertical	meunakh'	מאונך
very	meod'	מאוד
very bad	ra meod'	רע מאוד
very cheap	zol meod'	זול מאוד
very clean	naki' meod'	נקי מאוד
very close	karov' meod'	קרוב מאוד
very close connection	ke'sher haduk'	קשר הדוק
very good	tov meod'	טוב מאוד
very slowly	leat' leat'	לאט לאט
very well, fine	metsuyan'	מצוין
victory	nitsakhon'	ניצחון
video	vi'deo	ווידאו
view (n.)	reiya'	ראיה
vigorously	beme'rets	במרץ
village	kfar	כפר
vine	ge'fen	גפן
vinegar	kho'metz	חומץ
vineyard	ye'kev	יקב
violent	alim'	אלים
virus	vi'rus	וירוס
visa	vi'za	ויזה
visibility	re"ut'	ראות
vision	reiya'	ראיה
visit (n.)	bikur'	ביקור
visit (v.)	levaker'	לבקר
vitamin (vitamins)	vitamin' (vitamin'im)	ויטמין (ויטמינים)
vodka	vod'ka	וודקה

voice	kol	קול
volleyball	kadur"af'	כדורעף
vote (n.)	hatsbaa'	הצבעה
voter (voters)	matsbi'a (matsbiim')	מצביע (מצביעים)
voyage	haflaga'	הפלגה

W

wait (v.)	lekhakot'	לחכות
wait a minute	khake' re'ga	חכה רגע!
waiter	meltsar'	מלצר
wake up	lehit"orer'	להתעורר
walk (v.)	lale'khet	ללכת
wall	kir	קיר
wall closet	aron' kir	ארון קיר
want (v.)	lirtsot'	לרצות
wanted	mevukash', darush'	מבוקש, דרוש
war	milkhama'	מלחמה
warm	kham	חם
was	haya'	היה
wash (v.)	lirkhots'	לרחוץ
wash the laundry	lekhabes' et hakvisa'	לכבס את הכביסה
wash up	lehitrakhets'	להתרחץ
washing machine	mekhonat' kvisa'	מכונת כביסה
waste of time	bizbuz' zman	בזבוז זמן
watch (n.)	shaon'	שעון
watch (v.)	lishmor'	לשמור
water	ma'im	מים
watermelon	avati'yakh	אבטיח
wave (n.)	gal	גל
way	de'rekh	דרך
we	anakh'nu	אנחנו
weak (m.)	khalash'	חלש
weak (f.)	khalasha'	חלשה
wealthy	amida'	עמידה
weapon	kley ne'shek	כלי נשק
weather	me'zeg avir'	מזג אויר
Wednesday	yom rvii'	יום רביעי
week	shavu'a	שבוע
weight	mishkal'	משקל
welcome!	barukh' haba'!	ברוך הבא!
weld (v.)	leratekh	לרתך
welding	ritukh'	ריתוך
welding machine	rate'khet	רתכת
welfare	rvakha'	רווחה
well (adv.)	tov	טוב
west	maarav'	מערב
wet	ratuv'	רטוב
what?	ma?	מה?
when?	matay'?	מתי?

where?	ey'fo, heykhan'?	איפה, היכן?
which? (m.)	ey'ze?	איזה?
which? (f.)	ey'zo?	איזו?
which? (pl.)	ey'lu?	אילו?
while (conj.)	beod'	בעוד
white (m.)	lavan'	לבן
white (f.)	levana'	לבנה
white cheese	gvina' levana'	גבינה לבנה
white wine	ya'in lavan'	יין לבן
who?	mi?	מי?
whoever	mi she...	מי ש...
whole	shalem'	שלם
why?	la'ma?	למה?
wide (m.)	rakhav'	רחב
wide (f.)	rekhava'	רחבה
width	ro'khav	רוחב
wife	raaya'	רעיה
wild (adj.)	paru'a	פרוע
wind	ru'akh	רוח
window	khalon'	חלון
windshield wiper	magav'	מגב
windy	yesh ru'akh	יש רוח
wine	ya'in	יין
winter	kho'ref	חורף
wise (m.)	khakham'	חכם
wise (f.)	khakhama'	חכמה
wish (n.)	ratson'	רצון
with	im	עִם
withdraw	nesiga'	נסיגה
within	betokh'	בתוך
without	bli	בלי
wolf	ze'ev	זאב
woman	isha'	אשה
wonder (n.)	pe'le	פלא
wonderful	nehedar'	נהדר
wonderful feeling	hargasha' metsuye'net	הרגשה מצוינת
wood	ets	עץ
wool	tse'mer	צמר
word	mila'	מילה
world	olam'	עולם
work (v.)	laavod'	לעבוד
work (works)	avoda' (avodot')	עבודה (עבודות)
worker	poel'	פועל
workers union	igud' ovdim'	איגוד עובדים
worry (n.)	daaga'	דאגה
worthwhile	shave', keday'	שווה, כדאי
wound (n.)	pe'tsa	פצע
wounded	nifga', patsu'a	נפגע, פצוע
write	likhtov'	לכתוב
writer	sofer'	סופר

written by	meet′	מאת
wrong	lo nakhon′	לא נכון

X

xerox	haatakat′ she′mesh, tsilum′ mismakhim′	העתקת שמש, צילום מיסמכים
x ray	tsilum′ rentgen′	צילום רנטגן

Y

year	shana′	שנה
year 2,000	shnat alpa′im	שנת 2000
yellow (m.)	tsahov′	צהוב
yellow (f.)	tsehuba′	צהובה
yellow cheese	gvina′ tsehuba′	גבינה צהובה
yes	ken	כן
yes, indeed	omnam′ ken	אמנם כן
yes, of course	ken, kamuvan′	כן, כמובן
yesterday	etmol′	אתמול
yet	od, ada′in	עוד, עדיין
yield	knia′	כניע
yogurt	le′ben	לבן
you (m.)	at	אתה
you (f.)	ata′	את
you can′t rely on it	i-efshar′ lismokh′	אי אפשר לסמוך
you have no right	eyn lekha′ rshut′	אין לך רשות
you never know	i-efshar′ lada′at	אי אפשר לדעת
you paid cash	shilam′ta bemezuman′	שלמת במזומן
you see!	ata′ roe′!	אתה רואה!
you should know	ratsu′y sheteda′	רצוי שתדע
you want?	rotse′?	רוצה?
young (m.)	tsair′	צעיר
young (f.)	tseira′	צעירה
your question	sheelatkha′	שאלתך
your, yours (m.)	shelkha	שלך
your, yours (f.)	shelakh′	שלך
youth hostel	akhsaniyat′ no′ar	אכסניית נוער

Z

zero	e′fes	אפס
zombie	go′lem	גולם
zone	ezor′	איזור
zoo	gan khayot′	גן חיות

HEBREW PHRASEBOOK

1. INTRODUCTIONS

English	Transliteration	Hebrew
How are you? (m.)	**ma shlomkha'?**	מה שלומך?
(f.)	**ma shlomekh'?**	מה שלומך?
How are you? (m.)	**ma itkha'?**	מה איתך?
(f.)	**ma itakh'?**	מה איתך?
How is he (she)?	**eykh hu (hi)?**	איך הוא (היא)?
What's your name? (m.)	**ma shimkha'?**	מה שמך?
(f.)	**ma shmekh?**	מה שמך?
My name is...	**shmi...**	שמי...
Where are you from? (m.)	**mie'yfo ata'?**	מאיפה אתה?
(f.)	**mie'yfo at?**	מאיפה את?
I'm from New York.	**ani' minyu' york.**	אני מניו יורק.
How did you get here? (pl.)	**eykh higa'tem?**	איך הגעתם?
by plane	**bematos'**	במטוס
by bus	**beo'tobus**	באוטובוס
by ship	**besfina'**	בספינה
on the night flight	**betisat' la'yla**	בטיסת לילה
How do you feel? (m.)	**eykh ata margish'?**	איך אתה מרגיש?
(f.)	**eykh at margisha'?**	איך את מרגישה?
How is everything?	**ma hainyanim?**	מה הענינים?
How are things?	**ma nishma'?**	מה נשמע?
age	**gil**	גיל
How old are you?		
(m.)	**ben ka'ma ata'?**	בן כמה אתה?
(f.)	**bat ka'ma at?**	בת כמה את?

2. ETIQUETTE

Shalom!	**shalom'!**	שלום!
How are things?	**ma nishma'?**	מה נשמע?
Fine, thanks.	**toda' bese'der.**	תודה בסדר.
Good morning.	**bo'ker tov.**	בוקר טוב.
Good evening.	**e'rev tov.**	ערב טוב.
Good night.	**lay'la tov.**	לילה טוב.
Sabbath greetings.	**Shabat' shalom'.**	שבת שלום.
Happy New Year.	**shana' tova'.**	שנה טובה.
Happy holidays.	**khag same'yakh.**	חג שמח.
Happy birthday.	**yom hole'det same'yakh.**	יום הולדת שמח.
With God's help.	**beezrat' hashem'.**	בעזרת השם.
Thank God.	**barukh' hashem'.**	ברוך השם.
I'm fine.	**shlomi' tov.**	שלומי טוב.
Bye, see you soon.	**lehitraot'.**	להתראות.
Call me!	**titkasher' elay'!**	תתקשר אלי!
I'll call you.	**ani' etkasher' ele'kha.**	אני אתקשר אליך.
Have a good time.	**biluy' naim'.**	בילוי נעים.
Welcome.	**barukh' haba'.**	ברוך הבא.
Welcome. (pl.)	**brukhim' habaim'.**	ברוכים הבאים.
Yes.	**ken.**	כן.
No.	**lo.**	לא.
Thanks.	**toda'.**	תודה.
Good luck!	**behatslakha'!**	בהצלחה!
Excuse me!	**slikha'!**	סליחה!
Can I?	**efshar'?**	אפשר?
I'm sorry.	**ani mitstaer'.**	אני מצטער.
Please.	**bevakasha'.**	בבקשה.

ETIQUETTE

Sure!	**be'takh!**	בטח!
Are you sure?	**batu'akh?**	בטוח?
With pleasure.	**beratson'.**	ברצון.
Nevertheless...	**bekhol'zot...**	בכל זאת...

• EXCLAMATION WORDS

God forbid!	**khas vekhali'la!**	חס וחלילה!
Oh my God!	**oy vaavoi' li!**	אוי ואבוי לי!
A pity (that)...	**khaval' she...**	חבל ש...
Come on, let's	**ha'va**	הבה
May it be	**halevay'**	הלוואי
Of course!	**vaday', bevaday'!**	ודאי, בודאי!
Perfect!	**metsuyan'!**	מצוין!
Please.	**bevakasha'.**	בבקשה.
Quiet!	**she'ket!**	שקט!
Really?!	**bekhaye'kha?!**	בחייך?!
Really! Sure!	**bekhayay'!**	בחיי!
Very well.	**tov meod'.**	טוב מאוד.
Well.	**tov.**	טוב.
Without a doubt	**bli safek'**	בלי ספק
Wonderful, great	**nehedar', yo'fi**	נהדר, יופי

3. QUICK REFERENCE

I want... (m.)	**ani'rotse'...**	אני רוצה...
(f.)	**ani'rotsa'...**	אני רוצה...
I don't want... (m.)	**ani' lo rotse'...**	אני לא רוצה...
(f.)	**ani' lo rotsa'...**	אני לא רוצה...
I know. (m.)	**ani' yode'a.**	אני יודע.
(f.)	**ani' yoda'at.**	אני יודעת.
I don't know. (m.)	**ani' lo yode'a.**	אני לא יודע.
(f.)	**ani' lo yoda'at.**	אני לא יודעת.
You are right. (m.)	**ata' tsode'k.**	אתה צודק.
(f.)	**at tsode'ket.**	את צודקת.
You are wrong. (m.)	**ata' lo tsodek'.**	אתה לא צודק.
(f.)	**at' lo tsodeket'.**	את לא צודקת.
I'm sorry. (m.)	**ani' mitstaer'.**	אני מצטער.
(f.)	**ani' mitstaeret'.**	אני מצטערת.
Do you (m.) understand?	**ata' mevin'?**	אתה מבין?
(f.)	**at mevina'?**	את מבינה?
You (m.) don't understand.	**ata' lo mevin'.**	אתה לא מבין.
(f.)	**at' lo mevina'.**	את לא מבינה.
I (m.) don't understand you.	**ani' lo mevin' otkha'.**	אני לא מבין אותך.
(f.)	**ani' lo mevin' otakh'.**	אני לא מבין אותך.
I (m.) don't understand you.	**ani' lo mevina' otkha'.**	אני לא מבינה אותך.
(f.)	**ani' lo mevina' otakh'.**	אני לא מבינה אותך.
Thank you, thank you.	**toda', toda'.**	תודה, תודה.
Thank you very much.	**toda' raba'.**	תודה רבה.

QUICK REFERENCE

Here is...	**kan nimtsa'...**	כאן נמצא...
It's important.	**ze khashuv'.**	זה חשוב.
It's interesting.	**ze mean"yen'.**	זה מענין.
It's nothing!	**ze klum!**	זה כלום!
No problem!	**eyn baaya'!**	אין בעיה!
No choice.	**eyn brera'.**	אין ברירה.
This, please.	**bevakasha' et ze.**	בבקשה את זה.
That's it.	**ze hakol'.**	זה הכל.
Is everything o.k.?	**hakol' bese'der?**	הכול בסדר?
very good	**tov meod'**	טוב מאוד
very bad	**ra meod'**	רע מאוד
o.k.	**bese'der**	בסדר
Help me!	**azru' li!**	עזרו לי!
It's dangerous.	**ze mesukan'.**	זה מסוכן.
How does one say...?	**eykh omrim'...?**	איך אומרים...?
I do not speak Hebrew. (m.)	**ani' lo medaber' ivrit'.**	אני לא מדבר עברית.
(f.)	**ani' lo medabe'ret ivrit'.**	אני לא מדברת עברית.
I do not understand Hebrew. (m.)	**ani' lo mevin' ivrit'.**	אני לא מבין עברית.
(f.)	**ani' lo mevina' ivrit'.**	אני לא מבינה עברית.
I'm...	**ani'...**	אני...
hungry.	**raev'.**	רעב.
tired.	**ayef'.**	עייף.
satisfied.	**merutse'.**	מרוצה.
disappointed.	**meukhzav'.**	מאוכזב.
traveling.	**nose'a.**	נוסע.
staying.	**nish"ar'.**	נשאר.
flying back.	**tas khazara'.**	טס חזרה.
This is a, an...	**ze...**	זה...
a lot.	**harbe'.**	הרבה.
a little.	**meat', ktsat.**	מעט, קצת.

a bit.	**tipa'.**	.טיפה
incorrect, wrong.	**lo nakhon'.**	.לא נכון
It is not possible.	**lo yitakhen'.**	.לא יתכן
It is possible.	**yitakhen'.**	.יתכן
just, only	**stam**	סתם
less	**pakhot'**	פחות
like	**kmo, ki.../ke...**	...כמו, כ
like this (m.)	**kaze'**	כזה
(f.)	**kazot'**	כזות
little, a little	**ktsat**	קצת
many, much	**harbe'**	הרבה
more	**yoter'**	יותר
no, not	**lo**	לא
not exactly	**lo bediyuk'**	לא בדיוק
not so good	**lo kol kakh'**	לא כל כך
not so much	**lo kol kakh**	לא כל כך
nothing	**klum, meuma', shum davar'**	כלום, מאומה, שום דבר
once	**pa'am**	פעם
otherwise	**akhe'ret**	אחרת
perhaps	**ulay'**	אולי
possible	**efshar'**	אפשר
quickly	**maher'**	מהר
really?	**haomnam'?**	?האומנם

4. INQUIRIES

When's the flight?	**matay' hatisa'?**	מתי הטיסה?
What's the flight number?	**ma mispar' hatisa'?**	מה מספר הטיסה?
Departure time has changed.	**zman hahamraa' shuna'.**	זמן ההמראה שונה.
Flight arrival at...	**hanekhita' beshaa'...**	הנחיתה בשעה...
final	**sofi'**	סופי
not final	**lo sofi**	לא סופי
Who?	**mi?**	מי?
What?	**ma?**	מה?
Where?	**ey'fo?**	איפה?
Where to?	**lean'?, leey'fo?**	לאן?, לאיפה?
Where from?	**meey'fo?**	מאיפה?
When?	**matay'?**	מתי?
Which? (m.)	**ey'ze?**	איזה?
Which? (f.)	**ey'zo?**	איזו?
Why?	**la'ma?**	למה?
Why?	**madu'a?**	מדוע?
Why not?	**la'ma lo?**	למה לא?
How?	**eykh?**	איך?
How much? (many)	**ka'ma?**	כמה?
Who is this?	**mi' ze?**	מי זה?
Who is there (here)?	**mi ze sham (kan)?**	מי זה שם (כאן)?
Who are you?	**mi ata' (at)?**	מי אתה (את)?
Who is he (she)?	**mi hu (hi)?**	מי הוא (היא)?
Who's in favor?	**mi bead'?**	מי בעד?
Who's against?	**mi ne'ged?**	מי נגד?
Who's with us?	**mi ita'nu?**	מי אתנו?
Who's with you?		
(m.)	**mi itkha'?**	מי אתך?
(f.)	**mi itakh'?**	מי אתך?
whoever	**mi she...**	מי ש...

INQUIRIES

What?	**ma?**	מה?
What is this?	**ma ze?**	מה זה?
What for?	**bishvil' ma?**	בשביל מה?
What is this for?	**biglal' ma?**	בגלל מה?
What's this here (there)?	**ma ze kan (sham)?**	מה זה כאן (שם)?
What's with you?		
(f.)	**ma itkha'?**	מה אתך?
(m.)	**ma itakh ?**	מה אתך?
(m.)	**ma yesh lekha'?**	מה יש לך?
(f.)	**ma yesh lakh?**	מה יש לך?
What's this here?	**ma yesh kan (po)?**	מה יש כאן (פה)?
What do you want from me?		
(m.)	**ma ata' rotse' mime'ni?**	מה אתה רוצה ממני?
(f.)	**ma at rotsa' mimeni?**	מה את רוצה ממני?
What's happening here?	**ma kore' po (kan)?**	מה קורה פה (כאן)?
What are you writing? (m.)	**ma ata' kotev'?**	מה אתה כותב?
(f.)	**ma at kote'vet?**	מה את כותבת?
What are you reading? (m.)	**ma ata' kore'?**	מה אתה קורא?
(f.)	**ma at koret'?**	מה את קוראת?
What happened?	**ma kara'?**	מה קרה?
What happened to him, her?	**ma kara' lo, la?**	מה קרה לו, לה?
What do you see?		
(m.)	**ma ata' roe'?**	מה אתה רואה?
(f.)	**ma at roa'?**	מה את רואה?
What do you do?		
(m.)	**ma ata' ose'?**	מה אתה עושה?
(f.)	**ma at osa'?**	מה את עושה?
What do you feel? (m.)	**ma ata' margish'?**	מה אתה מרגיש?

(f.)	**ma at margisha'?**	מה את מרגישה?
What will there be?	**ma yihye' sham?**	מה יהיה שם?
What did you take?	**ma lakakh'ta?**	מה לקחת?
What do you need for...?	**ma ata' tsarikh' bishvil'...?**	מה אתה צריך בשביל...?
What's the matter?	**ma yesh?**	מה יש?
What do you care? (m.)	**ma ikhpat' lekha'?**	מה איכפת לך?
(f.)	**ma ikhpat' lakh?**	מה איכפת לך?
What do you intend to do?	**ma ata' mitkaven' laasot'?**	מה אתה מתכוון לעשות?
From what?	**mima'?**	ממה?
Where?	**ey'fo?**	איפה?
Where is it?	**ey'fo ze?**	איפה זה?
About where is it?	**ey'fo ze kan?**	איפה זה כאן?
Where is it located?	**ey'fo ze nimtsa'?**	איפה זה נמצא?
Where will it be?	**ey'fo ze yihye'?**	איפה זה יהיה?
Where is it happening?	**ey'fo ze mitrakhesh' (kore')?**	איפה זה מתרחש (קורה)?
Where are you?		
(m.)	**ey'fo ata'?**	איפה אתה?
(f.)	**ey'fo at?**	איפה את?
Where are you? (pl.)	**ey'fo atem'?**	איפה אתם?
Where are they?	**ey'fo hem'?**	איפה הם?
Where is he?	**ey'fo hu?**	איפה הוא?
Where is he now?	**ey'fo hu nimtsa'?**	איפה הוא נמצא?

INQUIRIES

When?	**matay'?**	מתי?
When did this happen?	**matay' ze kara'?**	מתי זה קרה?
When will it be?	**matay' ze yih"ye'?**	מתי זה יהיה?
How much?	**ka'ma?**	כמה?
How much is it?	**ka'ma ze?**	כמה זה?
How much does it cost?	**ka'ma ze ole'?**	כמה זה עולה?
How much does it weigh?	**ka'ma ze shokel'?**	כמה זה שוקל?
How much do you need? (m.)	**ka'ma ata' tsarikh'?**	כמה אתה צריך?
(f.)	**ka'ma at tsrikha'?**	כמה את צריכה?
How much do you want? (m.)	**ka'ma ata' rotse'?**	כמה אתה רוצה?
(f.)	**ka'ma at rotsa'?**	כמה את רוצה?
How much is it altogether?	**ka'ma sakh ḥakol'?**	כמה סך הכל?
How long do I have to wait? (m.)	**ka'ma ani' tsarikh' lekhakot'?**	כמה אני צריך לחכות?
(f.)	**ka'ma ani' tsrikha' lekhakot'?**	כמה אני צריכה לחכות?
How?	**eykh?**	איך?
How is it?	**eykh ze?**	איך זה?
How are you? (m.)	**ma shlomkha'?**	מה שלומך?
How are you? (f.)	**ma shlomekh'?**	מה שלומך?
Which? (m.)	**ey'ze?**	איזה?
Which? (f.)	**ey'zo?**	איזו?
Which? (pl.)	**ey'lu?**	אילו?

INQUIRIES

From where?	**meey'fo, mea'yin?**	מאיפה, מאין?
Where is this from?	**meey'fo ze?**	מאיפה זה?
Why?	**la'ma?**	למה?
Why is that?	**la'ma ze?**	למה זה?
Why not?	**la'ma lo?**	למה לא?

5. LANGUAGE

Do you speak English? (m.)	**ata' medaber' anglit'?**	אתה מדבר אנגלית?
(f.)	**at medabe'ret anglit'?**	את מדברת אנגלית?
Does anyone here speak English?	**mishehu' kan medaber' anglit'?**	מי שהוא כאן מדבר אנגלית?
It's a dictionary.	**ze milon'.**	זה מילון.
Show me the word in Hebrew.	**har"e' li et hamila' beivrit'.**	הראה לי את המילה בעברית.
Say it to me in Hebrew.	**tagid' li et ze beivrit'.**	תגיד לי את זה בעברית.
How do you say it in Hebrew?	**eykh omrim' beivrit?**	איך אומרים בעברית?
Help me.	**azru' li.**	עזרו לי.
There's a translation in the phrasebook.	**yesh tirgum' basikhon'.**	יש תרגום בשיחון.
There's an index at the beginning.	**yesh pirut' nos"im' behatkhala'.**	יש פירוט נושאים בהתחלה.

6. FAMILY

This is a/an/the...		
(m.)	**ze...**	זה...
(f.)	**zot...**	זאת...
family.	**mishpakha'.**	משפחה.
my family.	**mishpakhti'**	משפחתי.
my wife.	**ishti'.**	אשתי.
husband.	**baal'.**	בעל.
my husband.	**baali'.**	בעלי.
father.	**av.**	אב.
my father.	**a'ba.**	אבא.
mother.	**em.**	אם.
my mother.	**i'ma sheli'.**	אמא שלי.
brother.	**akh.**	אח.
my brother.	**akhi'.**	אחי.
sister.	**akhot'.**	אחות.
my sister.	**akhoti'.**	אחותי.
children.	**yeladim'.**	ילדים.
son.	**ben.**	בן.
my son.	**bni.**	בני.
daughter.	**bat.**	בת.
my daughter.	**biti'.**	בתי.
grandson.	**ne'khed.**	נכד.
my grandson.	**ne'khed sheli'.**	נכד שלי.
granddaughter.	**nekhda'.**	נכדה.
my granddaughter.	**nekhda' sheli.**	נכדה שלי.
grandfather.	**sa'ba.**	סבה.
grandmother.	**sa'vta.**	סבתא.
uncle.	**dod.**	דוד.
my uncle.	**dod sheli'.**	דוד שלי.
aunt.	**do'da.**	דודה.
my aunt.	**dodati'.**	דודתי.
We're married.	**ana'khnu nesuim'.**	אנחנו נשואים.
I am single.	**ani' levad'**	אני לבד.

FAMILY

I am divorced. (m.)	**ani' garush'.**	אני גרוש.
(f.)	**ani grusha'.**	אני גרושה.
I am a widower.	**ani alman'.**	אני אלמן.
I am a widow.	**ani almana'.**	אני אלמנה.
son-in-law	**khatan'**	חתן
daughter-in-law	**kala'**	כלה
father-in-law	**khoten'**	חותן
mother-in-law	**khote'net**	חותנת
We are getting married.	**yesh la'nu khatuna'.**	יש לנו חתונה.

7. RELIGION & NATIONALITY

RELIGION

I'm...	**ani'...**	...אני
a Christian.	**notsri'.**	.נוצרי
a Jew.	**yehudi'.**	.יהודי
a Muslim.	**mu'slemi.**	.מוסלמי
He's...	**hu...**	...הוא
religious.	**dati'.**	.דָתִי
Orthodox.	**ortodoks'.**	.אורטודוקס
Reform Jewish.	**yehudi' refo'rmi.**	יהודי רפורמי.
Conservative Jew.	**yehudi konservati'vi.**	יהודי .קונסרבטיבי.
Catholic.	**kato'li.**	.קתולי
Protestant.	**protesta'nt.**	.פרוטסטנט
Anglican.	**anglika'ni.**	.אנגליקני

NATIONALITY

American	**amerika'i**	אמריקאי
Arab	**aravi'**	ערבי
Argentinian	**argentina'i**	ארגנטינאי
Australian	**ostra'li**	אוסטרלי
Belgian	**be'lgi**	בלגי
Brazilian	**barzila'i**	ברזילאי
Canadian	**kana'di**	קנדי
Chinese	**si'ni**	סיני
English	**angli'**	אנגלי
French	**tsorfati'**	צרפתי
German	**germani'**	גרמני
Indian	**ho'di**	הודי
Italian	**italki'**	איטלקי
Japanese	**yapa'ni**	יפני
Russian	**rusi'**	רוסי
Spanish	**sfaradi'**	ספרדי

8. TRANSPORTATION

A common form of public transport in Israel is the bus company called "Egged" - "אגד" operating in all parts of the country except for Tel Aviv. The "Dan" - "דן" company operates in the Tel Aviv area. The cost of a bus journey, in the city area, is a little over $1 per journey. Inter-city buses depart from the Central Bus Station, also called "Egged" - "אגד" in each town. Taxis operate all over the country and can be ordered by phone. The train operates between Tel Aviv, Haifa, Acco and Naharia.

BUYING TICKETS

Please give me	**ten li bevakasha'**	תן לי בבקשה
a ticket to...	**kartis' le'...**	כרטיס ל...
I need	**ani tsarich'**	אני צריך
a ticket...	**kartis'...**	כרטיס...
to Tel Aviv.	**letel'-aviv'.**	לתל אביב.
on a trip.	**latiyul'.**	לטיול.
abroad.	**lekhuts' laa'rets.**	לחוץ לארץ.
How much does	**ka'ma ole'**	כמה עולה
a one-way ticket	**cartis'**	כרטיס
to Jerusalem	**lirushala'im**	לירושלים
cost?	**kivun' ekhad'?**	כיוון אחד?
return?	**haloch' vashov'?**	הלוך ושוב?

AIR TRAVEL

I want	**ani' rotse'**	אני רוצה
to fly...	**latus'...**	לטוס...
tomorrow.	**makhar'.**	מחר.
in two days time.	**beod' yoma'im.**	בעוד יומיים.
With which company will I fly? (m.)	**bee'yzo khevra' ani' tas?**	באיזו חברה אני טס?
(f.)	**bee'yzo khevra' ani' ta'sa?**	באיזו חברה אני טסה?

TRANSPORTATION

What is the flight number?	**ma' mispar' hatisa'?**	מה מספר הטיסה?
When is the flight?	**matay' hatisa'?**	מתי הטיסה?
Are any business class tickets available?	**yesh kartisim' lemakhle'ket asakim'?**	יש כרטיסים למחלקת עסקים?
Are any tourist class tickets available?	**yesh kartisim' lemakhle'ket tayarim'?**	יש כרטיסים למחלקת תיירים?
When does the plane land?	**matay' hamatos' nokhet'?**	מתי המטוס נוחת?
Would it be possible to sit in the "smoking" area?	**efshar' lashe'vet beagaf' meashnim'?**	אפשר לשבת באגף מעשנים?
Would it be possible to sit in the "no-smoking" area?	**efshar' lashe'vet beagaf' halo' meashnim'?**	אפשר לשבת באגף הלא מעשנים?
Do you have kosher food?	**yesh lakhem' o'khel kasher'?**	יש לכם אוכל כשר?
How do I change my flight?	**eykh meshanim' et hatisa'?**	איך משנים את הטיסה?
How do I change the date of the flight?	**eykh meshanim' et taarikh' hatisa'?**	איך משנים את תאריך הטיסה?
How much does it cost?	**ka'ma ze ole'?**	כמה זה עולה?

BUS & TAXI

Where is the bus stop?	**e'yfo takhanat' o'tobus?**	איפה תחנת אוטובוס?
When will it arrive?	**matay' hu magi'a?**	מתי הוא מגיע?

TRANSPORTATION

English	Transliteration	Hebrew
How long is the journey to...	**ka'ma zman ad...**	כמה זמן עד...
Jerusalem?	**yerusahala'im?**	ירושלים?
Tiberias?	**tve'ria?**	טבריה?
Eilat?	**eylat'?**	אילת?
When's the next bus?	**matay' hao'tobus haba'?**	מתי האוטובוס הבא?
Please tell me when to get off.	**bevakasha' tagid' li e'yfo lare'det.**	בבקשה תגיד לי איפה לרדת.
I need "Emek Refaim" street.	**ani' tsarikh' rkhov' "e'mek refaim'".**	אני צריך רחוב "עמק רפאים".
Which bus goes there?	**ey'ze mispar' magi'a lesham'?**	איזה מספר מגיע לשם?
Where do I take bus number...?	**ey'fo ani' loke'yakh o'tobus mispar'...?**	איפה אני לוקח אוטובוס מספר...?
Where does the luggage go?	**ey'fo lasim' mizvadot'?**	איפה לשים מזוודות?
Where is the central bus station?	**eyfo' hatakhana' hamerkazit'?**	איפה התחנה המרכזית?
Where is...	**e'yfo...**	איפה...
"information"?	**hamodiin'?**	המודיעין?
taxi stand?	**takhanat' moniyot'?**	תחנת מוניות?
How much would it cost to take a taxi to the city center?	**ka'ma ola' monit' lamerkaz'?**	כמה עולה מונית למרכז?
How long is the journey?	**ka'ma zman nesiya'?**	כמה זמן נסיעה?
Take me...	**kakh' oti'...**	קח אותי...
to the airport.	**lenamal' teufa'.**	לנמל תעופה.

to this address.	**el hakto'vet hazot'.**	אל הכתובת הזאת.
Please stop!	**taatsor' bevakasha'!**	תעצור בבקשה!
Help me put in the luggage.	**taazor' li lehakhnis' et hamizvadot'.**	תעזור לי להכניס את המזוודות.
Help me take out the luggage.	**taazor' li lehotsi' et hamizvadot'.**	תעזור לי להוציא את המזוודות.
Thank you!	**toda'!**	תודה!

USEFUL WORDS

Where is...?	**ey'fo...?**	איפה...?
customs	**me'khes**	מכס
entrance	**knisa'**	כניסה
exit	**yetsia'**	יציאה
flight arrivals	**nekhitot'**	נחיתות
flight departures	**tisot' yots"ot'**	טיסות יוצאות
information	**modiin'**	מודיעין
Magen David *(emergency medical unit)*	**magen' david'**	מגן דוד
passport control	**biko'ret darkonim'**	ביקורת דרכונים
restrooms	**shirutim'**	שירותים
telephone	**te'lefon**	טלפון

9. THE CAR

It's not particularly enjoyable to drive in Israel, but it should be mentioned that the use of a private car allows you to more fully enjoy the wonderful sights of the Holy Land.

The roads are mostly narrow, winding, and, more often than not, blocked with traffic. Traffic signs and road markings are not clear; however, an English translation accompanies the Hebrew.

If you get stuck on a side road in the city and can't find the way to the center or a main road, we recommend the use of a map and planning the route beforehand. Maps are available at car rental agencies and bookstores.

The maximum speed limit on the inter-city roads is 80 km/hr unless otherwise indicated. 100 km/hr is only allowed on the Tel-Aviv – Jerusalem, Haifa – Tel-Aviv and Tel-Aviv – Ashdod highways. The city speed limit is 50 km/hr. Morning hours are usually full of traffic jams. Take special care at "cross-walks" – sometimes both pedestrians and vehicles have a green light.

Have your car documents ready when stopped by traffic police.

Where can I rent a car?	**ey'fo sokhrim' re'khev?**	איפה שוכרים רכב?
I would like to rent a car. (m.)	**hayiti' rotse' liskor' re'khev.**	היתי רוצה לשכור רכב.
I am having problems with...	**yesh li baaya' im...**	יש לי בעיה עם...
Can you fix...?	**ata' yakhol' letaken'...?**	אתה יכול לתקן...?
brakes	**blamim'**	בלמים

THE CAR

battery	**matsber′**	מצבר
alternator	**alterna′tor**	אלטרנטור
steering wheel	**he′ge**	הגה
accelerator	**davshat′ gaz**	דוושת גז
clutch	**matsmed′**	מצמד
gear box	**tivat′ hilukhim′**	תיבת הילוכים
automatic gear box	**tivat′ hilukhim′ otoma′tit**	תיבת הילוכים אוטומטית
brights	**orot′ gvohim′**	אורות גבוהים
regular lights	**orot ktanim′**	אורות קטנים
parking lights	**orot′ khanaya′**	אורות חניה
indicator lights	**vin′kerim**	וינקרים
windshield wipers	**magavim′**	מגבים
sheet metal	**pakh**	פח
left side	**tsad smol**	צד שמאל
right side	**tsad yamin′**	צד ימין
tire	**tsamig′**	צמיג
tires	**tsmigim′**	צמיגים
inner tube	**pnimit′**	פנימית
air pressure	**la′khats avir′**	לחץ אויר
puncture	**pan′cher, te′ker**	פנצ׳ר, תקר
speed	**mhirut′**	מהירות
gasoline	**de′lek**	דלק
gasoline station	**takhanat′ de′lek**	תחנת דלק
water	**ma′im**	מים
oil	**she′men**	שמן
radiator	**radia′tor**	רדיאטור

USEFUL WORDS

car	**mekhonit′**	מכונית
car test	**rishyon′ re′khev**	רשיון רכב
documents	**teudot′**	תעודות
driver	**nahag′**	נהג
driver's license	**rishyon′ nehiga′**	רשיון נהיגה
fine	**knas**	קנס

THE CAR

garage	**mosakh′**	מוסך
insurance	**bitu′akh**	ביטוח
no entry	**eyn knisa′**	אין כניסה
parking	**khanaya′**	חניה
paid parking	**khanaya′ betashlum′**	חניה בתשלום
passenger	**nose′a**	נוסע
rent-a-car companies	**khevrot′ haskarat′ re′khev**	חברות השכרת רכב
road	**kvish**	כביש
road accident	**teunat′ drakhim′**	תאונת דרכים
road sign	**tamrur′**	תמרור
road sign (triangle)	**meshulash′**	משולש
route	**de′rekh**	דרך
seat belt	**khagura′t betikhut′**	חגורת בטיחות
stop sign	**tamrur′ atsor′**	תמרור עצור
traffic police	**mishte′ret tnua′**	משטרת תנועה
vehicle	**re′khev**	רכב

10. ACCOMMODATION

AT THE HOTEL

English	Transliteration	Hebrew
I'm looking for...		
(m.)	**ani' mekhapes'...**	אני מחפש...
(f.)	**ani' mekhape'set...**	אני מחפשת...
a three-star hotel.	**malon' shlosha' kokhavim'.**	מלון שלושה כוכבים.
a youth hostel.	**akhsaniyat' no'ar.**	אכסניית נוער.
I need...	**ani tsarikh'...**	אני צריך...
a room...	**khe'der...**	חדר...
for the night.	**lela'yla.**	ללילה.
for two days.	**leyoma'im.**	ליומיים.
for a week.	**leshavu'a.**	לשבוע.
two rooms.	**sney khadarim'.**	שני חדרים.
Bed & Breakfast	**tsi'mer**	צימר
How much is...	**ka'ma ole'...**	כמה עולה...
a bed and a breakfast?	**lina' im arutkhat' bo'ker?**	לינה עם ארוחת בוקר?
full board?	**pension' male'?**	פנסיון מלא?
Do you have a restaurant?	**yesh lakchem' mis"ada'?**	יש לכם מסעדה?
How long are you staying?	**ka'ma zman ata' nish"ar'?**	כמה זמן אתה נשאר?
I want to order in advance.	**ani rotse' lehazmin' makom' mirosh'.**	אני רוצה להזמין מקום מראש.
Do you have air-conditioning?	**yesh lakhem' mizug'avir'?**	יש לכם מיזוג אויר?
There is no electricity.	**eyn khashmal'.**	אין חשמל.
Is it a quiet room?	**hakhed'er shaket'?**	החדר שקט?
Is it far from the center?	**ze rakhok' mehamerkaz'?**	זה רחוק מהמרכז?

ACCOMMODATION

How much does a telephone call cost from the hotel?	**ka'ma ola' sikhat' te'lefon mehamalon'?**	כמה עולה שיחת טלפון מהמלון?
Where are...	**ey'fo...**	איפה...
the keys?	**hamaftekhot'?**	המפתחות?
my luggage?	**hamizvadot' sheli?**	המזוודות שלי?

NEEDS

I need...	**ani' tsarich'...**	אני צריך...
housekeeping.	**sherut' khadarim'.**	שירות חדרים.
toilet paper.	**n"yar' tualet'.**	נייר טואלט.
soap.	**sabon'.**	סבון.
hot water.	**ma'im khamim'.**	מים חמים.
drinking water.	**mey shtiya'.**	מי שתיה.
a map of the city.	**mapa' shel ha'ir.**	מפה של העיר.
How do you open the window?	**eych potkhim' khalon'?**	איך פותחים חלון?
How do I operate the air-conditioning unit?	**eych maf"ilim' mazgan'?**	איך מפעילים מזגן?
I'm checking out today.	**ani ozev' hayom'.**	אני עוזב היום.
The air-conditioning doesn't work.	**mizug' lo oved'.**	מיזוג לא עובד.

USEFUL WORDS

armchair	**kursa'**	כורסה
bath	**amba'tiya**	אמבטיה
bed	**mita'**	מיטה
blanket	**smikha'**	שמיכה

chair	**kise'**	כיסה
clean (adj.)	**naki'**	נקי
clothes closet	**aron' bgadim'**	ארון בגדים
cold water	**ma'im karim'**	מים קרים
dirty	**melukhlakh'**	מלוכלך
electricity	**khashmal'**	חשמל
hot water	**ma'im khamim'**	מים חמים
flowers	**prakhim'**	פרחים
lamp	**menora'**	מנורה
laundry	**kvisa'**	כביסה
lightbulb	**nura'**	נורה
pillow	**karit'**	כרית
rag	**smartut'**	סמרטוט
robe	**khaluk'**	חלוק
service	**shirut'**	שירות
sheets	**sdinim'**	סדינים
shower	**mikla'khat**	מקלחת
slippers	**naaley' bayt**	נעלי בית
television	**televi'ziya**	טלוויזיה
tip	**te'sher**	תשר

(It's usually enough to give a 5 shekel tip.)

towel	**mage'vet**	מגבת
video	**vi'deo**	ווידאו

11. DIRECTIONS

English	Transliteration	Hebrew
Where is...?	**e'yfo nimza'...?**	איפה נמצא...?
Please show me...	**tar'e' li bevakasha'...**	תראה לי בבקשה...
where is it?	**e'yfo ze?**	איפה זה?
how to get to...	**eych lehagi'a le...**	איך להגיע ל...
How do you get to....?	**eykh megiim' el...?**	איך מגיעים אל...?
Is it...?	**ze...?**	זה...?
It is...	**ze...**	זה...
far.	**rakhok'.**	רחוק.
close.	**karov'.**	קרוב.
straight down this street.	**yashar' barekhov' haze'.**	ישר ברחוב הזה.
two bus stops from here.	**shtey takhanot' o'tobus mikan'.**	שתי תחנות אוטובוס מכאן.
in that building.	**babinyan' hahu'.**	בבניין ההוא.
I don't know (m.), ask someone else.	**lo yode'a, tish"al' mi'shehu akher'.**	לא יודע, תשאל מישהו אחר.
(to) where...	**leey'fo/lean'...**	לאיפה/לאן...
Where are you going? (m.)	**lean' ata' holekh'?**	לאן אתה הולך?
(f.)	**lean' at hole'khet?**	לאן את הולכת?
Where do you plan to go? (m.)	**lean' ata' mitkaven' lale'khet?**	לאן אתה מתכוון ללכת?
(f.)	**lean' at mitkave'net lale'khet?**	לאן את מתכוונת ללכת?

DIRECTIONS

Where do you need to go? (m.)	**lean′ ata′ tsarikh′?**	לאן אתה צריך?
(f.)	**lean′ at tsrikha′?**	לאן את צריכה?
Where is this bus going?	**lean′ nose′a hao′tobus haze′?**	לאן נוסע האוטובוס הזה?
Ready? (m.)	**mukhan′?**	מוכן?
(f.)	**mukhana′?**	מוכנה?
I′m ready.	**ani mukhan′.**	אני מוכן.
Wait, I′m not ready yet. (m.)	**khake′ ani′ od lo mukhan′.**	חכה, אני עוד לא מוכן.
(f.)	**khake′ ani′ od lo mukhana′.**	חכה, אני עוד לא מוכנה.
Come here already. (m.)	**bo kvar.**	בוא כבר.
Come here. (f.)	**bo′i.**	בואי.
Where is a (an)...	**ey′fo kan...**	איפה כאן...
grocery?	**mako′let?**	מכולת?
supermarket?	**supermar′ket?**	סופרמרקט?
restaurant?	**mis"ada′?**	מסעדה?
coffee shop?	**beyt kafe′?**	בית קפה?
clinic?	**kupat′ kholim′?**	קופת חולים?
dentist?	**rofe′ shina′im?**	רופא שיניים?
bus?	**o′tobus?**	אוטובוס?
hotel?	**malon′?**	מלון?
bank?	**bank?**	בנק?
school?	**beyt se′fer?**	בית ספר?
kindergarten?	**gan yeladim′?**	גן ילדים?
nursery?	**peuton′?**	פעוטון?
store?	**khanut′?**	חנות?
market?	**shuk?**	שוק?
police?	**mishtara′?**	משטרה?
my group?	**hakvutsa′ sheli′?**	הקבוצה שלי?
information	**modiin′**	מודיעין
my friends	**hayedidim′**	הידידים
There.	**sham.**	שם.

DIRECTIONS

It's there.	**ze sham.**	זה שם.
Here.	**kan, po.**	כאן, פה.
Somewhere.	**eyfo' shehu'.**	איפה שהוא.
It's...	**ze...**	זה...
in this direction.	**bekivun' haze'.**	בכיוון הזה.
straight.	**yashar'.**	ישר.
to the left.	**smo'la.**	שמאלה.
to the right.	**yami'na.**	ימינה.
behind...	**akharey'...**	אחרי...
around...	**mesaviv'...**	מסביב...
above.	**lema'la.**	למעלה
backwards.	**akho'ra, leakhor'.**	אחורה, לאחור.
below.	**lema'ta.**	למטה.
farther.	**ha'l"a.**	הלאה.
forward.	**kadi'ma.**	קדימה.
from a distance.	**mirakhok'.**	מרחוק.
from above.	**milema'la.**	מלמעלה.
from below.	**milema'ta.**	מלמטה.
from where?	**mea'yin?**	מאין?
here	**he'na**	הנה
there	**lesham'**	לשם
where to?	**lean'?**	לאן?
where	**ey'fo, heykhan'**	איפה, היכן
It is located...	**ze nimtsa'...**	זה נמצא...
in the center of the town.	**bamerkaz' hair'.**	במרכז העיר.
in the room.	**bakhe'der.**	בחדר.
on the corner.	**bapina'.**	בפינה.
around the corner.	**mesaviv' lapina'.**	מסביב לפינה.
in the street.	**barkhov'.**	ברחוב.

DIRECTIONS

USEFUL WORDS

down	**lema'ta**	למטה
emergency exit	**yetsiat' kherum'**	יציאת חרום
entry	**knisa'**	כניסה
entry on duty	**knisa' betafkid'**	כניסה בתפקיד
exit	**yetsia'**	יציאה
forward	**kadi'ma**	קדימה
left	**smo'la**	שמאלה
return	**khazara'**	חזרה
right	**yami'na**	ימינה
stop	**atsor'**	עצור
street	**rkhov'**	רחוב
there	**lesham'**	לשם
to	**le...**	ל...
turn around	**tistovev'**	תסתובב
up	**lema'la**	למעלה

12. FOOD & DRINK

The tip in restaurants is usually about 10% of the bill.

Are you the waiter?	**ata' meltsar'?**	אתה מלצר?
Are you the waitress?	**at meltsari't?**	את מלצרית?
Menu, please.	**tafrit' bevakasha'.**	תפריט בבקשה.
Would it be possible to see the menu?	**efshar' lir"ot' tafrit'?**	אפשר לראות תפריט?
Could I have the menu please?	**tafrit' bevakasha'?**	תפריט בבקשה?
Is this an oriental restaurant?	**zot mis"ada' mizrakhit'?**	זאת מסעדה מזרחית?
Who is the manager?	**mi hamenahel'?**	מי המנהל?
Please give us (m.) the bill.	**tavi' la'nu kheshbon' bevakasha'.**	תביא לנו חשבון בבקשה.
(f.)	**tavi'i la'nu kheshbon' bevakasha.**	תביאי לנו חשבון בבקשה.
Everything is fine!	**hakol' bese'der!**	הכול בסדר!
Sorry!	**mitstaer'!**	מצטער!
Please clean the table.	**tenake'et hashulchan' bevakasha'.**	תנקה את השולחן בבקשה.
Please replace this dish.	**takhlif' li et hamana' bevakasha'.**	תחליף לי את המנה בבקשה.

It's not cooked!	**ze lo mevushal'!**	זה לא מבושל!
It tastes awful!	**ze lo taim'!**	זה לא טעים!
It's very tasty!	**taim' meod'!**	טעים מאוד!
It's spoiled!	**ze mekulkal'!**	זה מקולקל!
It's too sweet!	**ze matok' miday'!**	זה מתוק מידי!
It's too salty!	**ze malu'akh miday'!**	זה מלוח מידי!
It's not hot enough!	**ze lo kham!**	זה לא חם!
There isn't enough sauce.	**khaser' ro'tev.**	חסר רוטב.
Do you have...	**yesh lakhem'...**	יש לכם ...
sauce for the fish?	**ro'tev ledag'?**	רוטב לדג?
ketchup?	**ketchup'?**	קטצ'ופ?
Could you change...? (m.)	**ata' yakhol' lehakhlif'?**	אתה יכול להחליף?
(f.)	**at yakhola' lehakhlif'?**	את יכולה להחליף?
We would like to order...	**ana'khnu mazminim'...**	אנחנו מזמינים...
a first course.	**mana' rishona'.**	מנה ראשונה.
a second course.	**mana' shniya'.**	מנה שניה.
a main course.	**mana' ikarit'**	מנה עיקרית
a side dish.	**tose'fet.**	תוספת.
What does it taste like?	**ey'ze ta'am yesh lo?**	איזה טעם יש לו?
meat	**basar'**	בשר
meat (kosher)	**basari'**	בשרי
milk	**khalav'**	חלב
dairy (kosher)	**khalavi'**	חלבי
bread	**le'khem**	לחם
salad	**salat'**	סלט
salt	**me'lakh**	מלח

FOOD & DRINK

pepper	**pi'lpel**	פלפל
sugar	**sukar'**	סוכר
vinegar	**kho'metz**	חומץ
barley	**grisim'**	גריסים
cake	**uga'**	עוגה
breakfast	**arukhat' bo'ker**	ארוחת בוקר
lunch	**arukhat' tsohora'yim**	ארוחת צהריים
dinner	**arukhat' e'rev**	ארוחת ערב
yellow cheese	**gvina' tshuba'**	גבינה צהובה
white cheese	**gvina' levana'**	גבינה לבנה
sour cream	**shame'net**	שמנת
leben } different types of yoghurt	**le'ben**	לבן
eshel } different types of yoghurt	**e'shel**	אשל
egg	**beytsa'**	ביצה
fried egg	**khavita'**	חביתה
oil	**she'men**	שמן
butter	**khem"a'**	חמאה
soup	**marak'**	מרק
patties	**ktsitsot'**	קציצות
chicken	**of**	עוף
turkey	**ho'du**	הודו
roast	**tsli'**	צלי
steak	**stek'**	סטיק
frankfurter	**naknikiya'**	נקניקיה
rice	**o'rez**	אורז
fish	**dagim'**	דגים
pickled fish	**dag malu'akh**	דג מלוח
salami	**naknik'**	נקניק
french fries	**tchips**	ציפס
felafel	**fala'fel**	פלאפל
roasted meat in pita	**shvar'ma**	שוורמה
jam	**riba'**	ריבה
vegetables	**yerakot'**	ירקות
beet	**se'lek**	סלק
cabbage	**kruv**	כרוב

carrot	**ge'zer**	גזר
corn	**ti'ras**	תירס
cucumber	**melafefon'**	מלפפון
eggplant	**khatsilim'**	חצילים
olives	**zeytim'**	זיתים
onion	**batsal'**	בצל
pepper	**pilpel'**	פלפל
potatoes	**tapukhey' adama'**	תפוחי אדמה
squash	**kishuim'**	קישואים
tomato	**agvaniya'**	עגבניה
fruit	**perot'**	פרות
apple	**tapu'akh**	תפוח
banana	**bana'na**	בננה
grapefruit	**eshkolit'**	אשכולית
grapes	**anavim'**	ענבים
melon	**melon'**	מלון
orange	**tapuz'**	תפוז
peach	**afarsek'**	אפרסק
pear	**agas'**	אגס
plum	**shezif'**	שזיף
tangerine, oranges	**klemanti'not**	קלמנטינות
watermelon	**avati'yakh**	אבטיח
nuts	**egozim'**	אגוזים
sunflower seeds	**gar"inim'**	גרעינים
ice cream	**gli'da**	גלידה
beverages	**shtiya'**	שתיה
raspberry drink	**pe'tel**	פטל
Cola	**ko'la**	קולה
Tempo	**tem'po**	טמפו
Kinley	**kin'li**	קינלי
water	**ma'im**	מים
cold water	**ma'im karim'**	מים קרים
mineral water	**ma'im minera'liim**	מים מינרליים
tea	**te**	תה
coffee	**kafe'**	קפה

instant coffee	**nes kafe'**	נס קפה
vodka	**vod'ka**	וודקה
cognac	**ko'nyak**	קוניק
brandy	**bran'di**	ברנדי
wine	**ya'in**	יין
milk	**khalav'**	חלב
beer	**bi'ra**	בירה
malt beer	**bi'ra shkhora'**	בירה שחורה
table wine	**ya'in shulkhan'**	יין שולחן
red wine	**ya'in adom'**	יין אדום
white wine	**ya'in lavan'**	יין לבן
...juice	**mitz...**	מיץ...
apple	**tapukhim'**	תפוחים
orange	**tapuzim'**	תפוזים
grape	**anavim'**	ענבים
raspberry	**pe'tel**	פטל
lemon	**limon'**	לימון
I am a vegetarian	**ani' tsimkhoni'**	אני צמחוני
I eat kosher only.	**ani' okhel' rak kasher'.**	אני אוכל רק כשר.
I am allergic to...	**ani' ale'rgi le...**	אני אלרגי ל...

USEFUL WORDS

chair	**kise'**	כסא
cookies	**ugiyot'**	עוגיות
cup	**kos**	כוס
dish	**tsala'khat**	צלחת
fork	**mazleg'**	מזלג
knife	**sakin'**	סכין
mug	**se'fel**	ספל
napkin	**mapit**	מפית
oven	**tanur'**	תנור
refrigerator	**mekarer'**	מקרר
table	**shulkhan'**	שולחן
tablespoon	**kaf**	כף
teaspoon	**kapit'**	כפית

13. WHAT'S TO SEE

Do you have...	**yesh lakhem'...**	יש לכם...
a map?	**mapa'?**	מפה?
an English guide?	**hadrakha' beanglit'?**	הדרכה באנגלית?
I want to visit...	**ani' rotse' levaker'...**	אני רוצה לבקר...
the north.	**batsafon'.**	בצפון.
the south.	**badarom'.**	בדרום.
the Negev.	**bane'gev.**	בנגב.
the Dead Sea.	**beyam' hame'lakh.**	בים המלח.
Eilat.	**beeylat'.**	באילת.
How does one get to...	**eych magiim' le..**	איך מגיעים ל...
Jerusalem.	**yerushala'im.**	ירושלים.
the Old City.	**ir haatika'.**	עיר העתיקה.
Jaffa Gate.	**sha'ar ya'fo.**	שער יפו.
Damascus Gate.	**sha'ar shkhem.**	שער שכם.
Nazareth.	**natse'ret.**	נצרת.
Bethlehem.	**beyt' le'khem.**	בית לחם.
Where do you want to go?	**lean' ata'rotse' lale'khet?**	לאן אתה רוצה ללכת?
I would like to go... (m.)	**ani' rotse' lalekhet'...**	אני רוצה ללכת...
(f.)	**ani' rotsa' lalekhet'...**	אני רוצה ללכת...
to synagogue.	**labeyt' kne'set.**	לבית כנסת.
to the Temple Mount.	**lahar' haba'it.**	להר הבית.
to the Church of the Holy Sepulchre.	**laknesiyat ' hake'ver.**	לכנסיית הקבר.
to the Church of the Nativity.	**laknesiyat' hamolad'.**	לכנסיית המולד.

to the Western Wall.	**lako'tel.**	.לכותל
What shall we do this evening?	**ma osim' bae'rev?**	מה עושים בערב?
Are there...	**yesh...**	...יש
concerts?	**konser'tim?**	קונצרטים?
Is there...	**mu'sika**	מוסיקה
classical music?	**klas'it?**	קלאסית?
a discotheque?	**di'skotek**	דיסקוטק
a night club?	**moadon' la'yla**	מועדון לילה
dancing?	**rikudim'**	ריקודים
an art exhibition?	**taarukhat' tsiyurim'**	תערוכת ציורים
Where is...?	**eyfo' ze...?**	איפה זה...?
Israel Museum?	**muzeon' israel'?**	מוזיאון ישראל?
the Rockefeller Museum?	**muzeon' ro'kfeler?**	מוזיאון רוקפלר?
a movie?	**se'ret?**	סרט?
an exhibition?	**taarukha'?**	תערוכה?
a fashion show?	**tetsugat' ofna'?**	תצוגת אופנה?
a casino?	**kazi'no?**	קזינו?

14. COMMUNICATIONS

TELEPHONE

Dial 144 for Bezek Information to get a complete telephone listing.

Where is ...	**ey'fo yesh kan...**	...איפה יש כאן
a telephone?	**te'lephone?**	?טלפון
Area code for...	**hakido'met shel...**	הקידומת של...
Jerusalem (02).	**yerushala'im (02).**	.(02) ירושלים
Tel Aviv (03).	**tel aviv' (03).**	.(03) ת"א
the North (04).	**tsafon' (04).**	.(04) צפון
the South (07).	**darom' (07).**	.(07) דרום
Nazareth (06).	**natse'ret (06).**	.(06) נצרת
How much does a minute cost?	**ka'ma ola' daka'?**	?כמה עולה דקה
by public telephone	**bete'lefon tsiburi'**	בטלפון ציבורי
How do you make a call abroad?	**eykh mitkashrim' lekhul'?**	?איך מתקשרים לחו"ל
I can dial...	**ani' yakhol' lekhayeg'...**	אני יכול לחייג...
direct.	**khiyug' yashir'.**	.חיוג ישיר
It's busy.	**ze tafus'.**	.זה תפוס
It's a busy tone.	**yesh tslil mekuta'.**	.יש צליל מקוטע
It's call waiting.	**zo sikha' mamtina'.**	.זו שיחה ממתינה
What's the fax number?	**ma mispar' hafaks'?**	?מה מספר הפקס
What's your e-mail address?	**ma' hai'meyl shelakhem'?**	?מה האי-מייל שלכם

COMMUNICATIONS

How much does a cellular phone cost?	**ka’ma ole’ telefon’ selular’ri?**	כמה עולה טלפון סלולרי?
How much does it cost to rent a phone from... company?	**ka’ma ole’ liskor’ telefon’ selula’ri mikhevrot’...?**	כמה עולה לשכור טלפון סלולרי מחברות...?
Pelephone	**pe’lefon**	פלאפון
Cellcom	**se’lkum**	סלקום
Orange	**o’rangz**	אורנג׳
How much is one minute of airtime?	**ka’ma ola’ dakat’ avir’... ?**	כמה עולה דקה אויר...?
abroad	**lekhul’**	לחו״ל
inside Israel	**betokh’ israel’**	בתוך ישראל
Can you wrap it?	**efshar’ leeroz?**	אפשר לארוז?
Do you have a telephone directory?	**yesh se’fer telefo’nim?**	יש ספר טלפונים?

MAIL

mail	**do’ar**	דואר
How much does it cost to send a letter to America?	**ka’ma ole’ mikhtav’ leame’rika?**	כמה עולה מכתב לאמריקה?
How much does a parcel cost?	**ka’ma ola’ hakhavila’?**	כמה עולה החבילה?
What’s the weight limit to send by...	**ad ey’ze mishkal’ efshar’ lishlo’akh...**	עד איזה משקל אפשר לשלוח...
airmail?	**bedo’ar avir’?**	בדואר אויר?
surface mail?	**bedo’ar yam?**	בדואר ים?
I want to buy some stamps.	**ani rotse’ liknot’ bulim’.**	אני רוצה לקנות בולים.

15. BUREAUCRACY

English	Transliteration	Hebrew
Name.	**shem.**	שם.
What's your name? (m.)	**ma shimkha'?**	מה שמך?
(f.)	**ma shmekh'?**	מה שמך?
My name is...Yosef.	**shmi yo'sef**	שמי יוסף
My last name is...	**shem hamishpakha' sheli'...**	שם המשפחה שלי...
Address.	**kto'vet.**	כתובת.
Date of birth.	**taarikh' leda'.**	תאריך לידה.
Nationality.	**leom'.**	לאום.
Age.	**gil.**	גיל.
How old are you? (m.)	**ben ka'ma ata'?**	בן כמה אתה?
(f.)	**bat ka'ma at'?**	בת כמה את?
Here it is written that I am...	**kan katuv' sheani'...**	כאן כתוב שאני...
I am forty. (m.)	**ani ben arbaim'.**	אני בן 40.
I am thirty. (f.)	**ani bat sloshim'.**	אני בת 30.
Male.	**zakhar'.**	זכר.
Female.	**nekeva'.**	נקבה.
Religion.	**dat.**	דת.
Reason for visiting Israel:	**sibat' habikur' beisrael':**	סיבת הביקור בישראל:
business	**asakim'**	עסקים
tourist	**tayar'**	תייר
work	**avoda'**	עבודה
personal	**ishi'**	אישי
relatives	**krovey' mishpakha'**	קרובי משפחה
vacation	**khufsha'**	חופשה
Date.	**taarikh'.**	תאריך.
Entry date.	**taarikh' knisa'.**	תאריך כניסה.
Exit date.	**taarikh' yetsia'.**	תאריך יציאה.
Passport.	**darkon'.**	דרכון.

BUREAUCRACY

Passport number.	**mispar' darkon'.**	מספר דרכון.
Visa.	**vi'za.**	ויזה.
No stamp.	**eyn khote'met.**	אין חותמת.
You have to	**tsarikh'**	צריך
sign...	**lakhtom'...**	לחתום...
here.	**kan.**	כאן.
below.	**lema'ta.**	למטה.
You have	**tsarikh'**	צריך
to pay...	**leshalem'...**	לשלם...
a tax.	**mas.**	מס.
a fine. (penalty)	**knas.**	קנס.
Pass, please.	**taavor' bevakasha'.**	תעבור בבקשה.
Next in line, please.	**haba'betor' bevakasha'.**	הבא בתור בבקשה.
Papers/ documents.	**teudot'.**	תעודות.
Luggage.	**mit"an'.**	מטען.
Suitcase.	**mizvada'.**	מזוודה.
Ministry of the Interior.	**misrad' hapnim'.**	משרד הפנים.
Ministry of Tourism.	**misrad' hatayarut'.**	משרד התיירות.
Documents.	**mismakhim'.**	מסמכים.
Authorization.	**ishur'.**	אישור.
Form.	**to'fes.**	טופס.
Fill in the form.	**lemale' tfasim'.**	למלא טפסים.
Expired.	**Pag to'kef.**	פג תוקף.
Everything is fine.	**hakol' bese'der.**	הכול בסדר.

16. MONEY & FINANCE

The currency in Israel is the shekel. There are 20, 50, 100, 200 shekel notes and also coins of 10 agurot, 50 agurot, 1 shekel (there are 100 agurot in one shekel), 5 shekels and 10 shekels. In hotels, shops and places of entertainment it is better to pay in shekels as the rate of exchange here is usually lower than at the bank. In public institutions payment is only made in shekels.

When does the bank open?	**matay' potkhim' et ha bank?**	מתי פותחים את הבנק?
Where can I change money?	**ey'fo makhlifim' ke'sef?**	איפה מחליפים כסף?
At the money changer.	**etsel' khalfan' ksafim'.**	אצל חלפן כספים.
How much does the dollar cost today?	**ka'ma hado'lar ole' hayom'?**	כמה הדולר עולה היום?
What's the rate of exchange today?	**ma sha'ar hakhalifin' hayom'?**	מה שער החליפין היום?
What's the commission?	**ma haamala'?**	מה העמלה?
Can I pay by credit card?	**efshar' leshalem' bekartis' ashray'?**	אפשר לשלם בכרטיס אשראי?
Can I pay by check?	**efshar' leshalem' bechek'?**	אפשר לשלם בציק?
What's written here?	**ma katuv' kan?**	מה כתוב כאן?
Can I have change...?	**efshar' lekabel' o'def...?**	אפשר לקבל עודף...?
in dollars	**bedolar'im**	בדולרים

in shekels	**beshkalim'**	בשקלים
in coins	**bematbeot'**	במטבעות
in notes, bills	**bestarot'**	בשטרות

17. SHOPPING

Israel caters to all the tourist's needs and wants: clothes, food, and souvenirs can be bought in shops and local markets. It is worth mentioning the rich and colorful market in the Old City of Jerusalem, where one can find olive-wood crosses, copper Hanukiot, Arab style dresses, Armenian ceramics and many souvenirs.

Bargaining is acceptable and recommended.

Where can I buy...?	**ey'fo ani' yakhol' liknot'...?**	איפה אני יכול לקנות...? ?
Where do they sell...? Where are sold...?	**ey'fo mokhrim'...?**	איפה מוכרים...?
May I help you? (m.)	**efshar laazor' lekha'?**	אפשר לעזור לך?
(f.)	**efshar laazor' lakh?**	אפשר לעזור לך?
I am just looking, thank you.	**ani' rak mistakel', toda'.**	אני רק מסתכל, תודה.
Can you help me find a dress in my size?	**ata' yakhol' laazor' li limtso' simla' bamida' sheli'?**	אתה יכול לעזור לי למצוא שמלה במידה שלי?
I'd like to buy a hat.	**hai'ti rotse' liknot' ko'va.**	הייתי רוצה לקנות כובע.
May I try this shirt on?	**efshar' limdod' et hakhultsa' hazot'?**	אפשר למדוד את החולצה הזאת?
Where is the fitting room?	**eyfo' modedim'?**	איפה מודדים?

SHOPPING

Does this shirt come in other colors?	**yesh tsvaim′ akherim′ lakhultsa′?**	יש צבעים אחרים לחולצה?
It′s too...	**ze... miday′.**	זה...מידי.
big.	**gadol′.**	גדול.
small.	**katan′.**	קטן.
long.	**arokh′.**	ארוך.
short.	**katsar′.**	קצר.
I will need this in a bigger/ smaller size.	**ani′ tsarikh′ mida′ gdola′/ ktana′ yoter′.**	אני צריך מידה גדולה/ קטנה יותר.
Do you make alterations here?	**osim′ po tikunim′?**	עושים פה תיקונים?
Is there anything on sale?	**yesh mashehu′ bemivtsa′?**	יש משהו במבצע?
May I return this?	**ani′ yakhol′ lehakhzir′ et ze?**	אני יכול להחזיר את זה?
Can I pay with my credit card?	**efshar′ leshlem′ bekartis′ ashray?**	אפשר לשלם בכרטיס אשראי?
Every item in the store is on sale.	**hakol′ bemivtsa′.**	הכול במבצע.
The fitting room is this way.	**modedim′ sham.**	מודדים שם.
Our tailor will make all the necessary alterations.	**hatofer′ shela′nu y′ase et kol hatikunim′ hanekhutsim′.**	התופר שלנו יעשה את כול התיקונים הנחוצים.
We do not accept credit cards, cash only.	**lo mokhrim′ bekartis′ ashray′, rak bamezuman′.**	לא מוכרים בכרטיס אשראי, רק במזומן.

We accept returned items only if you have the receipt.	**ana'khnu mekablim' bekhazara' rak im hakabala'.**	אנחנו מקבלים בחזרה רק עם הקבלה.
How much does it cost?	**ka'ma ze ole'?**	כמה זה עולה?
It's...	**ze...**	זה...
expensive.	**yakar'.**	יקר.
cheap.	**zol.**	זול.
inexpensive.	**lo yakar'.**	לא יקר.
very cheap.	**zol meod'.**	זול מאוד.
I don't need anything.	**ani' lo tsarikh' shum davar'.**	אני לא צריך שום דבר.

USEFUL WORDS

despite	**af al pi she..., lamrot'**	אף על פי ש..., למרות
do you?	**haim'?**	האם?
enough	**maspik'**	מספיק
exactly	**bediyuk'**	בדיוק
few, a few	**meat'**	מעט
for naught	**lashav'**	לשווא
free	**khinam', bekhinam'**	חינם, בחינם
the most	**hakhi'**	הכי
there is no need	**eyn tso'rekh**	אין צורך
there isn't, there is no	**eyn**	אין
therefore	**al ken', lakhen'**	על כן, לכן
together	**ya'khad**	יחד
twice	**paama'im**	פעמיים
very	**meod'**	מאוד
yes	**ken**	כן

SHOPPING

CLOTHES, SHOES & ACCESSORIES

What do they sell in the store?	**ma mokhrim' bakhanut'?**	מה מוכרים בחנות?
clothes	**bgadim'**	בגדים
sweater	**sve'der**	סוודר
skirt	**khatsait'**	חצאית
shirt	**khultsa'**	חולצה
T-shirt	**khultsa' ktsara'**	חולצה קצרה
pants	**mikhnasa'im**	מכנסיים
belt	**khagura'**	חגורה
shorts	**shor'tim**	שורטים
stockings	**garbey' nay'lon**	גרבי ניילון
socks	**garba'im**	גרביים
shoes	**naala'im**	נעליים
scarf	**tsaif'**	צעיף
hat	**ko'va**	כובע
tie	**aniva'**	עניבה
bow tie	**anivat' parpar'**	עניבת פרפר
gloves	**kfafot'**	כפפות
shoelaces	**srukhim'**	שרוכים
sunglasses	**mishkafey' she'mesh**	משקפי שמש
sneakers	**naaley' sport**	נעלי ספורט
sport clothes	**bigdey' sport**	בגדי ספורט
casual dress	**lvush yom-yomi'**	לבוש יומיומי
full dress	**lvush khagigi'**	לבוש חגיגי
suit	**khalifa'**	חליפה
evening gown	**simlat' e'rev**	שמלת ערב
wedding dress	**simlat' kala'**	שמלת כלה
large sizes	**midot' gdolot'**	מידות גדולות
bathing suit	**be'ged yam**	בגד ים
beach sandals	**sandalim'**	סנדלים
cosmetics	**tamrukim'**	תמרוקים
souvenirs	**mazkerot'**	מזכרות
camera	**matslema'**	מצלמה
film	**se'ret**	סרט

photo	**tsilum′**	צילום
bookstore	**khanut′ sfarim′**	חנות ספרים
book	**sefer′**	ספר
newspaper	**iton′**	עיתון
notebook with	**makhbe′ret im**	מחברת עם
pencils	**efronot′**	עפרונות
ticket	**kartis′**	כרטיס
for the show	**lehatsaga′**	להצגה
for the movie	**lese′ret**	לסרט
food	**mazon′**	מזון
Where will the	**e′yfo yih"ye′**	איפה יהיה
trip be?	**hatiyul′?**	הטיול?
in Jerusalem.	**birushala′im.**	בירושלים.
in the Galilee.	**bagalil′.**	בגליל.
in Jordan.	**beyarden′.**	בירדן.
in Egypt.	**bemitsra′im.**	במצרים.
Can I...?	**ani′ yakhol′...?**	אני יכול...?
buy	**liknot′**	לקנות
choose	**livkhor′**	לבחור
drink	**iishtot′**	לשתות
eat	**leekhol′**	לאכול
try on	**limdod′**	למדוד
pay	**leshalem′**	לשלם
prefer	**lehaadif′**	להעדיף
to lengthen	**lehaarikh′**	להאריך
to shorten	**lekatser′**	לקצר

USEFUL WORDS

bakery	**maafiya′**	מאפיה
butcher	**itliz′**	אטליז
delicatessen shop	**maadaniya′**	מעדנייה
fishmonger	**mokher dagim′**	מוכר דגים
greengrocer	**yarkan′**	ירקן
grocery store	**mako′let**	מכולת
jeweler	**takhshitan′**	תכשיטן

SHOPPING

shop selling dairy products	**khanut' mozrey' khalav'**	חנות מוצרי חלב
newsstand	**dukhan' itonim'**	דוכן עיתונים
perfumery	**khanut' tamrukim'**	חנות תמרוקים
pharmacy	**beyt merka'khat**	בית מרקחת
shop	**khanut'**	חנות
souvenir store	**khanut' mazkarot'**	חנות מזכרות
stationer's	**khanut' makhshirey' ktiva'**	חנות מכשירי כתיבה
tailor	**khayat'**	חייט
tobacconist	**khanut' tabak'**	חנות טבק
watchmaker	**shaan'**	שען

18. TOOLS

Turn off. (m.)	**tisgor'.**	.תסגור
(f.)	**tisgeri'.**	.תסגרי
Turn on. (m.)	**tadlik'.**	.תדליק
(f.)	**tadli'ki.**	.תדליקי
Connect. (m.)	**tekhaber'.**	.תחבר
(f.)	**tekhabri'.**	.תחברי
I need... (m.)	**ani' tsarikh'...**	...אני צריך
(f.)	**ani tsrikha'...**	...אני ציכה
Can this be fixed?	**efshar' letaken' et ze?**	אפשר לתקן את זה?
How do you use this?	**eykh mishtamshim' beze?**	איך משתמשים בזה?
tools	**kelim'**	כלים
tool	**kli**	כלי
hammer	**patish'**	פטיש
nail	**masmer'**	מסמר
nails	**masmerim'**	מסמרים
screwdriver	**mavreg'**	מברג
pliers	**pla'yer**	פלייר
nut 9nuts)	**um (u'mim)**	אום (אומים)
screw (screws)	**bo'reg (bragim')**	בורג (ברגים)
saw	**masor'**	משור
electricity	**khashmal'**	חשמל
wire	**khut**	חוט
plug	**she'ka**	שקע
socket	**te'ka**	תקע
connection	**khibur'**	חיבור
disconnection	**ne'tek**	נתק
fuse	**ke'tser**	קצר
electrical outlet	**nekudat' khashmal'**	נקודת חשמל
color	**tse'va**	צבע
painting	**tsvia'**	צביעה

TOOLS

solvent	**memis'**	ממיס
brush	**mivre'shet**	מברשת
drill	**makdekha'**	מקדחה
drill bit	**makde'yakh**	מקדח
machine	**mekhona'**	מכונה
microscope	**mikroskop'**	מיקרוסקופ
materials	**khomarim'**	חומרים
leather	**or**	עור
tree	**ets**	עץ
metal	**mate'khet**	מתכת
steel	**plada'**	פלדה
iron	**barzel'**	ברזל
copper	**necho'shet**	נחושת
bronze	**arad'**	ארד
aluminum	**alumi'nium/ khamran'**	אלומיניום/ חמרן
tin	**bdil**	בדיל
zinc	**avats'**	אבץ
post	**mot**	מוט
tin	**pakh**	פח
plank	**ke'resh**	קרש
weld	**ritukh'**	ריתוך
welding machine	**rate'khet**	רתכת
solder	**halkhama'**	הלחמה
Personal Computer	**makhshev' ishi'**	מחשב אישי
screen, display	**masakh'**	מסך
keyboard	**makle'det**	מקלדת
modem	**mo'dem**	מודם
compact disc	**taklitor'**	תקליטור
memory	**zikaron'**	זיכרון
hardware	**khomra'**	חומרה
software	**tokhna'**	תוכנה
Internet	**in'ternet**	אינטרנט
bug	**bag**	באג
remote control	**shalat'**	שלט

19. HEALTH

I need...	**ani' tsarikh'...**	אני צריך...
to contact...	**lehitkasher'...**	להתקשר...
to call...	**likro' le...**	לקרוא ל...
to phone...	**letsaltsel'...**	לצלצל...
to see...	**lir'ot...**	לראות...
a doctor.	**rofe'.**	רופא.
a hospital.	**beyt kholim'.**	בית חולים.
an emergency medical unit.	**magen' david' adom'.**	מגן דוד אדום.
a nurse.	**akhot'.**	אחות.
medicine.	**trufa'.**	תרופה.
How do you feel? (m.)	**eykh ata' margish'?**	איך אתה מרגיש?
(f.)	**eykh at margisha'?**	איך את מרגישה?
I feel pain.	**ani' margish' keev'.**	אני מרגיש כאב.
I have...	**yesh li...**	יש לי...
a wound.	**pe'tsa.**	פצע.
a temperature.	**khom.**	חום.
He was unconscious.	**khu haya lelo' hakara'.**	הוא היה ללא הכרה.
What do you feel? (m.)	**ma ata' margish'?**	מה אתה מרגיש?
(f.)	**ma at margisha'?**	מה את מרגישה?
I'm perfectly fine.	**ani' bese'der gamur'.**	אני בסדר גמור.
I don't feel well.	**ani' lo margish' tov.**	אני לא מרגיש טוב.
I am pregnant.	**ani' beherayon'.**	אני בהריון.
I am allergic.	**yesh li aler'giya.**	יש לי אלרגיוה.
My... hurts.	**koev' li...**	כואב לי...
throat	**garon'**	גרון
head	**rosh**	ראש

HEALTH

hand	**yad**	יד
back	**gav**	גב
chest	**khaze'**	חזה
stomach	**be'ten**	בטן
knee	**be'rekh**	ברך
eye	**a'yin**	עין
ear	**o'zen**	אוזן
nose	**af**	אף
mouth	**pe**	פה
tongue	**lashon'**	לשון
teeth	**shina'im**	שיניים
skin	**haor'**	העור
heart	**lev**	לב
liver	**kaved'**	כבד
hand	**kaf hayad'**	כף היד
foot	**re'gel**	רגל
It hurts me here.	**koev' li kan.**	כואב לי כאן.

20. EMERGENCIES

English	Transliteration	Hebrew
Help!	**hatsi'lu!**	הצילו!
Can you help me? (m.)	**ata' yakhol' laazor' li?**	אתה יכול לעזור לי?
(f.)	**at yakhola' laazor' li?**	את יכולה לעזור לי?
Can I use your telephone? (m.)	**efshar' lehishtamesh' bate'lefon shelkha'?**	אפשר להשתמש בטלפון שלך?
Where is the nearest telephone?	**e'yfo hate'lefon hakarov'?**	איפה הטלפון הקרוב?
Does the phone work?	**hate'lefon oved?**	הטלפון עובד?
Who is in charge here?	**mi haakhrai' kan?**	מי האחראי כאן?
Call the police. (m.)	**tikra' lamishtara'.**	תקרא למשטרה.
(f.)	**tikrei' lamishtara'.**	תקראי למשטרה.
I'll call the police!	**ani ekra' lamishtara'!**	אני אקרא למשטרה!
Where is the police department?	**ey'fo hamishtara'?**	איפה המשטרה?
Please call a police officer.	**tikra' leshoter' bevakasha'.**	תקרא לשוטר בבקשה.
I need a lawyer.	**ani' tsarikh' o'rekh din.**	אני צריך עורך דין.
What's the law?	**ma omer' hakhok?**	מה אומר החוק?
Is it the prison?	**ze beyt hake'le?**	זה בית הכלא?
Is it the cell?	**ze ta hamaasar'?**	זה תא המאסר?

EMERGENCIES

They arrested me...	hem atsru' oti'...	הם עצרו אותי...
without any reason.	lelo' siba'.	ללא סיבה.
on accusation of...	beashma'...	באשמה...
on suspicion of...	bekha'shad shel...	בחשד של...
shoplifting.	gneva' mekhanut'.	גניבה מחנות.
drunk driving.	shenaha'gti shikor'.	שנהגתי שיכור.
Is there a doctor near here?	yesh kan rofe' basviva'?	יש כאן רופא בסביבה?
Call the doctor! (m.)	tikra' lerofe'!	תקרא לרופא!
Call the ambulance! (f.)	tikrei' lemagen' david'!	תקראי למגן דויד!
There's been an accident!	hayta' teuna'!	הייתה תאונה!
Is anyone hurt?	mishehu' niftsa'?	מישהו נפצע?
He was wounded in a road accident.	khu haya patsu'a beteunat' drakhim'.	הוא היה פצוע בתאונת דרכים.
Don't move!	lo lazuz'!	לא לזוז!
Go away! (m.)	lekh mipo'!	לך מפה!
(f.)	lekhi mipo'!	לכי מפה!
I am lost.	ani' avud'.	אני אבוד.
I've been raped.	ansu' oti'.	אנסו אותי.
Take me to the doctor.	kkhu' oti' lerofe'.	קחו אותי לרופא.
I've been robbed.	shadedu' oti'.	שדדו אותי.
Thief!	ganav'!	גנב!
I am not guilty.	ani' lo ashem'.	אני לא אשם.
I am innocent.	ani' khaf mipe'sha.	אני חף מפשע.

EMERGENCIES

My ... has been stolen.	**ganvu' li...**	גנבו לי...
I am afraid. (m.)	**ani' pokhed'.**	אני פוחד.
(f.)	**ani' pokhe'det.**	אני פוחדת.
How did it happen?	**eykh ze kara'?**	איך זה קרה?
Does anyone speak English?	**mi'shehu kan medaber' anglit'?**	מישהו כאן מדבר אנגלית?
Nothing is happening here.	**klum lo kore' kan.**	כלום לא קורה כאן.
All is quiet.	**hakol' shaket.'**	הכל שקט.
I want...	**ani' rotse'...**	אני רוצה...
to apply...	**lifnot' le...**	לפנות ל...
to get in touch...	**lehitkasher' le...**	להתקשר ל...
to call...	**likro' le...**	לקרוא ל...
my family.	**mishpakha' sheli'.**	משפחה שלי.
the American embassy.	**shagrirut' amerika'it.**	שגרירות אמריקאית.

USEFUL WORDS

murder	**re'tsakh**	רצח
need	**tsarikh'**	צריך
theft	**gneva'**	גניבה
to demand	**lidrosh'**	לדרוש
to know	**lada'at**	לדעת
to suspect	**lakhshod'**	לחשוד

21. SPORTS

Who won?	**mi nitsakh'?**	מי נצח?
Who's playing?	**mi mesakhek'?**	מי משחק?
What's the score at halftime?	**ma hatotsaa' shel hamakhatsit'?**	מה התוצאה של המחצית?
athletics	**atle'tika kala'**	אתלטיקה קלה
basketball	**kadursal'**	כדורסל
chess	**shakh**	שח
coach	**me'amen'**	מאמן
high jump	**kfitsa' el hago'va**	קפיצה אל לגובה
game	**miskhak'**	משחק
jumping	**kfitsot'**	קפיצות
ping pong	**te'nis shulkhan'**	טניס שולחן
soccer	**kadure'gel**	כדורגל
sprint	**ritsa'**	ריצה
swimming	**skhiya'**	שחיה
tennis	**te'nis**	טניס
volleyball	**kaduryad'**	כדור יד

22. POLITICS

The "Knesset" is the parliament of Israel. Once every four years the citizens of Israel elect parties to represent them in the Knesset. The Prime Minister is elected separately and he builds a government which remains in power until the following elections.
The government has to receive the approval of the Knesset after it has been established by the Prime Minister.
The Knesset sets the laws of the country and elects the President who is not involved in foreign or internal policy and acts mainly in a representative role.

Knesset	**kne'set**	כנסת
Knesset members	**khavrey' kne'set**	חברי כנסת
vote	**hatsbaa'**	הצבעה
government	**mimshala'**	ממשלה
President	**nasi'**	נשיא
Prime Minister	**rosh hamimshala'**	ראש הממשלה
Minister	**sar**	שר
Foreign Minister	**sar hakhuz'**	שר החוץ
conflict	**sikhsukh'**	סכסוך
war	**milkhama'**	מלחמה
front	**khazit'**	חזית
battle	**krav**	קרב
fire	**esh**	אש
bombing	**haftsatsa'**	הפצצה
soldiers	**khayalim'**	חיילים
wounded	**nifgaim'**	נפגעים
victory	**nitsakhon'**	ניצחון
defeat	**tvusa'**	תבוסה
withdraw	**nesiga'**	נסיגה

POLITICS

deportation of refugees	**geru'sh plitim'**	גירוש פליטים
peace	**shalom'**	שלום
peace agreement	**khoze' shalom'**	חוזה שלום
human rights	**zkhuyot' adam'**	זכויות אדם
law	**khok**	חוק
order	**se'der**	סדר
worker's union	**igud' ovdim'**	איגוד עובדים
party	**miflaga'**	מפלגה
movement	**tnua'**	תנועה
voters	**matsbiim'**	מצביעים
opposition	**mitnagdim'**	מתנגדים
supporters	**tomkhim'**	תומכים
newspapers	**itonim'**	עיתונים
press	**tikshor'ret**	תקשורת
government spokesperson	**dover' hamimshala'**	דובר הממשלה
demonstration	**hafgana'**	הפגנה
strike	**shvita'**	שביטה

23. FARMS & ANIMALS

FARMING

Agricultural farms in Israel comprise mainly kibbutz and moshav.

A kibbutz is a completely communal economic entity, where all facilities are shared by all of the members.

In a moshav, members own private farms and share in communal agricultural facilities. The lifestyle is similar to that of the European village.

In Arab villages, individuals generally own private farms.

mountain	**har**	הר
mound	**tel**	תל
kibbutz	**kibuts'**	קיבוץ
moshav	**moshav'**	מושב
house	**bayt'**	בית
garden	**gina'**	גינה
grass	**de'she**	דשא
irrigation	**hashkaya'**	השקיה
water sprinkler	**mamtera'**	ממטרה
lawn mower	**mekasa'khat de'she**	מכסחת דשא
orchard/citrus grove	**pardes'**	פרדס
vineyard	**ke'rem**	כרם
crop/yield	**yevul'**	יבול
path	**shvil**	שביל
field	**sade'**	שדה
green field	**sade' yarok'**	שדה ירוק
harvest	**katif'**	קטיף
grain crops	**tvua'**	תבואה
flower (flowers)	**pe'rakh (prakhim')**	פרח (פרחים)
tree (trees)	**ets (etsim')**	עץ (עצים)

FARMS & ANIMALS

olive (olives)	**za'it (zeytim')**	זית (זיתים)
olive trees	**atsey' za'it**	עצי זית
fruit	**perot'**	פרות
fruit trees	**atsey' pri**	עצי פרי
avocado	**avoka'do**	אבוקדו
bananas	**bana'not'**	בננות
vegetables	**yerakot'**	ירקות
grapefruit	**eshkoliyot'**	אשכוליות
oranges	**tapuzim'**	תפוזים
grapes	**ke'rem anavim'**	כרם ענבים
grape harvest	**batsir'**	בציר
vineyard	**ye'kev**	יקב
dairy	**makhleva'**	מחלבה
storeroom	**makhsan'**	מחסן
tractor	**tra'ktor**	טרקטור
inn	**pundak'**	פונדק
market	**shuk**	שוק
corner shop	**mako'let**	מכולת

ANIMALS

cow (cows)	**para' (parot')**	פרה (פרות)
sheep	**kvasim'**	כבשים
goats	**izim'**	עזים
dog (dogs)	**ke'lev (klavim')**	כלב (כלבים)
cat	**khatul'**	חתול
(cats)	**(khatulim')**	(חתולים)
mouse	**akhbar**	עכבר
(mice)	**(akhbarim')**	(עכברים)
horse (horses)	**sus' (susim')**	סוס (סוסים)
donkey	**khamor'**	חמור
camel	**gamal'**	גמל
wolf	**zeev'**	זאב
bird (birds)	**tsipor' (tsiporim')**	ציפור (ציפורים)
mosquito	**yetush**	יתוש
(mosquitoes)	**(yetushim')**	(יתושים)
fly (flies)	**zvuv (zvuvim')**	זבוב (זבובים)
fish (fish)	**dag (dagim')**	דג (דגים)

saltwater fish	**dagey' yam**	דגי ים
snake	**na'khash**	נחש
(snakes)	**(nakhashim')**	(נחשים)
scorpion	**akrab'**	עקרב
(scorpions)	**(akrabim')**	(עקרבים)
ant (ants)	**nemala'**	נמלה
	(nemalim')	(נמלים)

24. THE WEATHER

The weather in Israel is very hot during eight months of the year. The sun is so strong that special protection is required by wearing clothes that cover the whole body or by using a sunblock. Humidity is usually high in the coastal areas and lower in the Jerusalem area, Galilee and the Negev. During the winter, dress is the same as for autumn in Europe.

What is the temperature?	**ma hatemperatu'ra?**	מה הטמפרטורה?
Is it going to rain?	**yih"ye' ge'shem?**	יהיה גשם?
What will it be like tomorrow?	**ma me'zeg haavir' makhar'?**	מה מזג האוויר מחר?
Does it get cold at night?	**yih"ye' kar bala'yla?**	יהיה קר בלילה?
It's going to rain.	**yih"ye' ge'shem.**	יהיה גשם.
It's going to be...	**yih"ye'...**	יהיה...
rainy	**gashum'**	גשום
30 degrees in the shade.	**shloshim' maalot' batsel'.**	30 מעלות בצל.
strong wind	**ru'akh khazaka'**	רוח הזקה
hot desert wind	**khamsin'**	חמסין
hot, dry weather	**shara'v**	שרב
cold	**kar**	קר
dry	**yavesh'**	יבש
dust	**avak'**	אבק
hot	**kham**	חם
high humidity	**lakhut' gvoha'**	לחות גבוהה
rain	**ge'shem**	גשם
sun	**she'mesh**	שמש
weather	**me'zeg avir'**	מזג אויר
wind	**ru'akh**	רוח

You need... (m.)	**ata' tsarich'...**	אתה צריך...
(f.)	**at tsrikha'...**	את צריכה...
head covering	**kisuy' rosh**	כיסוי ראש
coat	**meil'**	מעיל
umbrella	**metriya'**	מטריה
You must drink a lot. (m.)	**ata' khayav' lishtot' harbe'.**	אתה חייב לשתות הרבה.
(f.)	**at' khaye'vet lishtot' harbe'.**	את חייבת לשתות הרבה.

25. NUMBERS

Numbers in Hebrew are different for masculine and feminine.

CARDINAL NUMBERS

Masculine:

one	**ekhad'**	אחד
two	**shna'im**	שניים
three	**shlosha'**	שלושה
four	**arbaa'**	ארבעה
five	**khamisha'**	חמישה
six	**shisha'**	שישה
seven	**shiv"a'**	שבעה
eight	**shmona'**	שמונה
nine	**tish"a'**	תשעה
ten	**asara'**	עשרה
eleven	**akhad' asar'**	אחד עשר
twelve	**shneim' asar'**	שנים עשר
thirteen	**shlosha' asar'**	שלושה עשר
fourteen	**arbaa' asar'**	ארבעה עשר
fifteen	**khamisha' asar'**	חמישה עשר
sixteen	**shisha' asar'**	שישה עשר
seventeen	**shiv"a' asar'**	שבעה עשר
eighteen	**shmona' asar'**	שמונה עשר
nineteen	**tish"a' asar**	תשעה עשר

Feminine:

one	**akhat'**	אחת
two	**shta'im**	שתיים
three	**shalosh'**	שלוש
four	**arba'**	ארבע
five	**khamesh'**	חמש
six	**shesh**	שש
seven	**she'va**	שבע
eight	**shmo'ne**	שמונה

nine	**tey'sha**	תשע
ten	**e'ser**	עשר
eleven	**akhat' esre'**	אחת עשרה
twelve	**shte'im esre'**	שתים עשרה
thirteen	**shlosh' esre'**	שלוש עשרה
fourteen	**arba' esre'**	ארבע עשרה
fifteen	**khamesh' esre'**	חמש עשרה
sixteen	**shesh esre'**	שש עשרה
seventeen	**shva esre'**	שבע עשרה
eighteen	**shmone' esre'**	שמונה עשרה
nineteen	**tsha' esre'**	תשע עשרה

Masculine & Feminine

twenty	**esrim'**	עשרים
twenty-one (m.)	**esrim' veekhad'**	עשרים ואחד
(f.)	**esrim' veakhat'**	עשרים ואחת
thirty	**shloshim'**	שלושים
forty	**arbaim'**	ארבעים
fifty	**khamishim'**	חמישים
sixty	**shishim'**	שישים
seventy	**shiv"im'**	שבעים
eighty	**shmonim'**	שמונים
ninety	**tish"im'**	תשעים
hundred	**me'a**	מאה
two hundred	**mata'im**	מאתים
three hundred	**shlosh meot'**	שלוש מאות
nine hundred	**tsha meot'**	תשע מאות
thousand	**e'lef**	אלף
two thousand	**alpa'im**	אלפיים
three thousand	**shlo'shet alafim'**	שלושת אלפים
seven thousand	**shiv"at' alafim'**	שבעת אלפים
ten thousand	**ase'ret alafim'**	עשרת אלפים
million	**mil"yon'**	מיליון

NUMBERS

ORDINAL NUMBERS

Masculine form

first	**rishon′**	ראשון
second	**sheni′**	שני
third	**shlishi′**	שלישי
fourth	**revii′**	רביעי
fifth	**khamishi′**	חמישי
sixth	**shishi′**	שישי
seventh	**shvii′**	שביעי
eighth	**shmini′**	שמיני
ninth	**tshii′**	תשיעי
tenth	**asiri′**	עשירי

Feminine form

first	**rishona′**	ראשונה
second	**shniya′**	שניה
third	**shlishit′**	שלישית
fourth	**reviit′**	רביעית
fifth	**khamishit′**	חמישית
sixth	**shishit′**	שישית
seventh	**shviit′**	שביעית
eighth	**shminit′**	שמינית
ninth	**tshiit′**	תשיעית
tenth	**asirit′**	עשירית

FRACTIONS

half	**khetsi′, makhatsit′**	חצי, מחצית
third	**shlish**	שליש
two-thirds	**shney′ shlish**	שני שליש
quarter	**re′va**	רבע
fifth	**khamishit′**	חמישית
sixth	**shishit′**	שישית
seventh	**shviit′**	שביעית
eighth	**shminit′**	שמינית
ninth	**tshiit′**	תשיעית

tenth	**asirit'**	עשירית
fifteenth	**khe'lek**	חלק
	hakhamisha'	החמישה
	asar'	עשר
hundredth	**meit'**	מאית
two hundredth	**shtey meiyot'**	שתי מאיות
thousandth	**alpit'**	אלפית
three	**shalosh'**	שלוש
thousandth	**alpiyot'**	אלפיות
three fifteenths	**shlolsha'**	שלושה
	khelkey'	חלקי
	khamisha' asar'	חמישה עשר
This adds up to...	**ze mitvasef' el...**	זה מתווסף אל...
I have counted ... number.	**ani' safa'rti ...**	אני ספרתי...
How many?	**ka'ma?**	כמה?

26. TIME & DATE

Day	**yom**	יום
on...	**be...**	ב...
Sunday	**yom rishon′;**	יום ראשון;
	yom a′lef	יום "א"*
Monday	**yom sheni′;**	יום שני;
	yom bet	יום "ב"*
Tuesday	**yom shlishi′;**	יום שלישי;
	yom gi′mel	יום "ג"*
Wednesday	**yom rvii′;**	יום רביעי;
	yom da′let	יום "ד"*
Thursday	**yom khamishi′;**	יום חמישי;
	yom hey	יום "ה"*
Friday	**yom shishi′;**	יום שישי;
	yom vav	יום "ו"*
Saturday/ Shabbat	**shabat′**	שבת

* These forms can be used interchangeably.

Month	**kho′desh**	חודש
January	**ya′nuar**	ינואר
February	**fe′bruar**	פברואר
March	**merts**	מרץ
April	**april′**	אפריל
May	**may**	מאי
June	**yu′ni**	יוני
July	**yu′li**	יולי
August	**o′gust**	אוגוסט
September	**septe′mber**	ספטמבר
October	**okto′ber**	אוקטובר
November	**nove′mber**	נובמבר
December	**detse′mber**	דצמבר
winter	**kho′ref**	חורף

summer	**ka'yts**	קיץ
spring	**aviv**	אביב
fall/autumn	**stav**	סתיו
Year	**shana'**	שנה
two years	**shnata'im**	שנתיים
three years	**shalosh' shanim'**	שלוש שנים
year 2,000	**shnat alpa'im**	שנת 2000
year...	**shnat...**	שנת...
2001	**alpa'im veakhat'**	2001
2002	**alpa'im ushta'im**	2002
2003	**alpa'im veshalosh'**	2003
morning	**bo'ker**	בוקר
afternoon	**tsohora'im**	צהריים
evening	**e'rev**	ערב
night	**la'yla**	לילה
hour	**shaa'**	שעה
minute	**daka'**	דקה
second	**shniya'**	שניה
What time is it?	**ma hashaa'?**	מה השעה?
I have no time.	**eyn li zman.**	אין לי זמן.
When do you want to do it? (m.)	**matay' ata' rotse' laasot' et ze?**	מתי אתה רוצה לעשות את זה?
(f.)	**matay' at rotsa' laasot' et ze?**	מתי את רוצה לעשות את זה?
When do you have time? (m.)	**matay' yesh lekha' zman?**	מתי יש לך זמן?
(f.)	**matay' yesh lakh zman?**	מתי יש לך זמן?
When are we meeting?	**matay' anakh'nu nifgashim'?**	מתי אנחנו נפגשים?

TIME & DATE

When is it over?	**matay' ze nigmar'?**	מתי זה נגמר?
Next week.	**bashavu'a haba'.**	בשבוע הבא.
On Friday evening.	**bee'rev shabat'.**	בערב שבת.
On Saturday evening.	**bemotsey' shabat'.**	במוצאי שבת.
When is the store open?	**matay' nifta'khat hekhanut'?**	מתי נפתחת החנות?
today	**hayom'**	היום
tomorrow	**makhar'**	מחר
yesterday	**etmol'**	אתמול
last night	**e'mesh**	אמש
the day before yesterday	**shilshom'**	שלשום
in the morning	**babo'ker**	בבוקר
in the evening	**bae'rev**	בערב
during the day	**bayom'**	ביום
at night	**balay'la**	בלילה
early	**mukdam'**	מוקדם
at one o'clock	**beshaa' akhat'**	בשעה אחת
at two o'clock	**beshaa' shta'im**	בשעה שתיים
at three o'clock	**beshaa' shalosh'**	בשעה שלוש
at four o'clock	**beshaa' ar'ba**	בשעה ארבע
at five o'clock	**beshaa' khamesh'**	בשעה חמש
at six o'clock	**beshaa' shesh'**	בשעה שש
at seven o'clock	**beshaa' she'va**	בשעה שבע
at eight o'clock	**beshaa' shmo'ne**	בשעה שמונה
at nine o'clock	**beshaa' te'sha**	בשע תשעה
at ten o'clock	**beshaa' e'ser**	בשעה עשר
at eleven o'clock	**beshaa' akhat' esre'**	בשעה אחת עשרה
at twelve o'clock	**beshaa' shteim' esre'**	בשעה שתים עשרה
at six thirty	**beshaa' shesh vakhe'tsi**	בשעה שש וחצי

at a quarter past six	**beshaa' shesh vare'va**	בשעה שש ורבע
at a quarter to six	**beshaa' re'va leshesh'**	בשעה רבע לשש
at six ten	**beshaa' shesh veasara'**	בשעה שש ועשרה
at twenty to seven	**beshaa' esrim' leshe'va**	בשעה עשרים לשבע
at ten to seven	**beshaa' asara' leshe'va**	בשעה עשרה לשבע
exactly on time	**bediyuk' bazman'**	בדיוק בזמן
early	**mukdam'**	מוקדם
late	**meukhar'**	מאוחר
when...	**kaasher'...**	כאשר...
before...	**lifney'...**	לפני...
after...	**akharey', leakhar'...**	אחרי, לאחר...
in...	**beod'...**	בעוד...
a day	**yom**	יום
two days	**yoma'im**	יומיים
three days	**shlosha yamim'**	שלושה ימים
four days	**arbaa' yamim'**	ארבעה ימים
five days	**khamisha' yamim'**	חמישה ימים
six days	**shisha' yamim'**	שישה ימים
a week	**shavu'a**	שבוע
two weeks	**shvua'im**	שבועיים
three weeks	**shlosha' shavuot'**	שלושה שבועות
after	**akharey'**	אחרי
afterwards	**akhar' kakh**	אחר כך
after New Year	**akharey' rosh hashana'**	אחרי ראש השנה
already	**kvar**	כבר
always	**tamid'**	תמיד
another time	**pa'am akhe'ret**	פעם אחרת
at first	**tkhila'**	תחילה

TIME & DATE

before	**lifney'**	לפני
before noon.	**lifney' hatsohora'im**	לפני הצהריים...
early	**mukdam'**	מוקדם
finally	**sof sof**	סוף סוף
first	**ko'dem**	קודם
forever	**leolam', letamid'**	לעולם, לתמיד
from then, since	**meaz'**	מאז
immediately	**miyad'**	מיד
in a while	**beod' zman ma**	בעוד זמן מה
in the end	**besofo' shel davar'**	בסופו של דבר
late	**meukhar'**	מאוחר
long ago	**mizman'**	מזמן
meanwhile	**beynta'im**	בינתיים
never	**af paam'**	אף פעם
now	**akhshav'**	עכשיו
often	**leitim' krovot'**	לעיתים קרובות
once	**pa'am**	פעם
rarely	**leitim' rekhokot'**	לעיתים רחוקות
recently	**lo mizman'**	לא מזמן
since when?	**mimatay'?**	ממתי?
sometimes	**lif"amim', leitim'**	לפעמים, לעיתים
soon	**bekarov'**	בקרוב
still, more	**od**	עוד
still, yet	**od, ada'in**	עוד, עדיין
suddenly	**pit"om'**	פתאום
then	**az**	אז
till evening	**ad hae'rev**	עד הערב
until when?	**ad matay'?**	עד מתי?
urgent	**dakhuf'**	דחוף
when?	**matay'?**	מתי?
until	**ad**	עד

27. COLORS

Which color...	**ey'ze tse'va...**	...איזה צבע
do you prefer?		
(m.)	**ata' maadif'?**	?אתה מעדיף
(f.)	**at maadifa'?**	?את מעדיפה
do you choose?		
(m.)	**ata' bokher'?**	?אתה בוחר
(f.)	**at bokhe'ret?**	?את בוחרת
suit you better?	**yat"im' lekha'**	יתאים לך
(m.)	**yoter'?**	?יותר
(f.)	**yat"im' lakh**	יתאים לך
	yoter'?	?יותר
color	**tse'va**	צבע
shade	**gavan'**	גוון
monotonous	**khadgoni'**	חדגוני
colorful	**tsiv"oni'**	צבעוני
dark	**kehe'**	כהה
light	**bahir'**	בהיר
deep	**amok'**	עמוק
black	**shakhor'**	שחור
blue	**kakhol'**	כחול
green	**yarok'**	ירוק
greenish	**yarakrak'**	ירקרק
grey	**afor'**	אפור
gold	**zahav'**	זהב
orange	**katom'**	כתום
pink	**varod'**	ורוד
red	**adom'**	אדום
reddish	**adamdam'**	אדמדם
transparent	**shakuf'**	שקוף
turquoise	**tkhe'let**	תכלת
white	**lavan'**	לבן
yellow	**tsahov'**	צהוב

28. PROFESSIONS

English		Transliteration	Hebrew
I am a/an...		**ani'...**	אני...
This is a.../an...		**ze...**	זה...
I used to be a/an...		**hayi'ti...**	הייתי...
I am retired.		**yatsa'ti lapen'siya.**	יצאתי לפנסיה.
My profession is...		**hamiktso'a sheli'...**	המקצוע שלי...
army officer	(m.)	**katsin'**	קצין
	(f.)	**ktsina'**	קצינה
clerk	(m.)	**pakid'**	פקיד
	(f.)	**pkida'**	פקידה
doctor	(m.)	**rofe'**	רופא
	(f.)	**rof"a'**	רופאה
driver	(m.)	**nahag'**	נהג נהגת
	(f.)	**nahe'get**	
electrician		**khashmalay'**	חשמלאי
engineer		**mehandes'**	מהנדס
guide	(m.)	**madrikh'**	מדריך
	(f.)	**madrikha'**	מדריכה
librarian		**safranit'**	ספרנית
mailman		**davar'**	דוור
manager	(m.)	**menahel'**	מנהל
nurse		**akhot'**	אחות
policeman	(m.)	**shoter'**	שוטר
	(f.)	**shote'ret**	שוטרת
porter		**sabal'**	סבל
programmer			
	(m.)	**metakhnet'**	מתכנת
	(f.)	**metakhne'tet**	מתכנתת
salesperson			
	(m.)	**mokher'**	מוכר
	(f.)	**mokhe'ret**	מוכרת
scientist	(m.)	**mad"an'**	מדען
	(f.)	**mad"anit'**	מדענית
secretary	(f.)	**mazkira'**	מזכירה

soldier	(m.)	**khayal'**	חייל
	(f.)	**khaye'let**	חיילת
student	(m.)	**student'**	סטודנט
	(f.)	**studen'tit**	סטודנטית
teacher	(m.)	**more'**	מורה
	(f.)	**mora'**	מורה
technician		**tekhnai'**	טכנאי
waiter		**meltsar'**	מלצר
waitress		**meltsarit'**	מלצרית
worker	(m.)	**poel'**	פועל
	(f.)	**poe'let**	פועלת

Other Hippocrene Titles of Regional and Cultural Interest

Sephardic Israeli Cuisine
260 pages • 6 x 9 • ISBN 0-7818-0926-6 • W • $24.95hc • 21

Israel: An Illustrated History
148 pages • 5½ x 8½ • ISBN 0-7818-0756-5 • W • $11.95hc • 24

1,401 Questions and Answers About Judaism
400 pages • 6 x 9 • ISBN 0-7818-0993-2 • W • $18.95pb • 547

Jewish First Names
126 pages • 5 x 7 • ISBN 0-7818-0727-1 • W • $11.95hc • 095

Under the Wedding Canopy: Love and Marriage in Judaism
243 pages • 6 x 9 • 0-7818-0481-7 • W • $22.50hc • 596

Zilberman's Hebrew-English/English-Hebrew Dictionary
Revised Edition
55,000 entries • 624 pages • 5 x 7 • 0-7818-0875-8 • W • $22.50pb • 236

English-Hebrew/Hebrew-English Conversational Dictionary
Revised Edition
7,000 entries • 160 pages • 5½ x 8½ • ISBN 0-7818-0137-0 • W • $9.95pb • 257

Dictionary of 1,000 Jewish Proverbs
131 pages • 5½ x 8½ • ISBN 0-7818-0529-5 • W • $11.95pb • 628

Yiddish-English/English-Yiddish Practical Dictionary
4,000 entries • 146 pages • 4¾ x 7 • 0-7818-0439-6 • W • $9.95pb • 431

Prices subject to change without notice. To purchase **Hippocrene Books**, contact your local bookstore, call (718) 454-2366, or write to: HIPPOCRENE BOOKS, 171 Madison Avenue, New York, NY 10016. Please enclose check or money order, adding $5.00 shipping (UPS) for the first book, and $.50 for each additional book.

www.ingramcontent.com/pod-product-compliance
Lightning Source LLC
Jackson TN
JSHW011400130125
77033JS00023B/767

* 9 7 8 0 7 8 1 8 0 8 1 1 8 *